D0206284

Feeding the Zircon Gorilla. . .
& Other Teambuilding Activities

Sam Sikes

Property of
Uinta County Extension Service
228 9th Street — Evanston, WY 82930
phone: (307) 783-0570

All rights reserved. No part of this book may be reproduced in any form or by any means without permission in writing from the publisher except as noted below. All inquiries should be addressed to Learning Unlimited Corporation, Tulsa, Oklahoma

Permission is granted to reproduce activity templates within this book.

Copyright© 1995 by Sam Sikes
ISBN 0-9646541-0-5

Learning Unlimited Corporation
5155 East 51st, Suite 108
Tulsa, OK 74135
(918) 622-3292   fax (918) 622-4203

Printed in the United States of America

Table of Contents

Matrix of Recommended Team Sizes

For Teams of:	2-4	5-8	9-13	14-19	20+
Balloon Castle		x	x	x	
Barbarian Golf	x	x	x		
Coin Flip, Inc.		x	x		
Compass Walk		x	x	x	
Don't Touch Me		x	x	x	x
Easy. . . Knot!				x	x
Feeding the Zircon Gorilla					x
Fing Fong Fooey	x	x	x	x	x
Giant Texas Lizard Egg		x	x		
The Great Nail Puzzle	x	x			
Grid (1, 2, & 3-way)		x	x	x	
Group Leader		x	x		
Gutterball		x	x		
Horizontal Spider Web		x	x	x	
House		x	x	x	
The Infinite Circle		x	x	x	
Lines of Communication		x	x		
On Target		x	x	x	x
Oogly	x	x	x	x	x
Photo Finish			x	x	x
Plastic Wrap		x	x	x	x
Portable Zig-Zag		x	x		
Puff-O-War	x	x			
Quality Journey		x	x		
Quick Mathematical Division			x	x	
Rock Scientists			x	x	
Sardines Scenario			x	x	x
Sorry Sucker		x	x	x	x
Star		x	x	x	
Strategic Tic Tac Toe	x	x			
Team Belay		x			
Team Blowgun		x	x		
Tower E.G.G. Drop	x	x	x		
Transporting Quality		x	x	x	
Trolley Journey		x	x		
Trust Scavenger Hunt	x	x			
Vortex with a Twist		x	x	x	x
Wampum			x	x	

Introduction

Why Write This Book?

This book has taken several years to create. The activities have been created for actual teams and customized for the various needs of many customers. My hope is that many training professionals can use the activities from this book and customize the activities to the specific needs of the teams they facilitate.

In truth, many of the activities we facilitate had never been written down. We would create these wild scenarios from the assessments of each team, offer the activity, and debrief the team's approach and solution. Many games and initiatives were very popular. The most popular I have written in this book.

At last, I can hand a trainer some instructions instead of trying to verbally describe all the rules and contingencies over the phone or on the way to a training session.

I have written before. I wrote my first book in the fifth grade. **X-Unknown** is a science fiction story about a man exiled from Earth and sent on a one-way mission to a newly discovered planet. My second book, **Indoor Games: For College Students and the Extremely Bored**, was written while I was still in college. The book includes a collection of competitive games my friends and I created in our dormitory. The first book was written at the request of my fifth grade teacher for a writer's exhibition. I wrote it in pencil and used map colors to draw illustrations. My mother typed the text for me and we bound it with glue and cloth. The second book I wrote with money in mind. I figured every college and university bookstore could use a few copies to sell. I did everything myself, writing, printing, cutting, binding, marketing and delivery. As of 1994, I have sold two dozen books. I have many requests for the book, but each book takes so long to assemble that it isn't worth it.

Now, as I type, I have already created the remainder of this book. My motivation for writing this latest book is again different from the previous two. I see catalogs of games and initiatives cross my desk several times a month. It seems that most of the activities have been around for many years and someone decides to give some of the best ones a face lift. The activities get new names in a slick publication so they can be used by another generation of trainers. I want to add some <u>new</u> activities to the pool.

How The Activities Evolved

Necessity <u>is</u> the mother of invention. Most of the activities in this book developed from a need to create a new activity to mirror a specific dynamic within a team. Some were specifically made for a particular team or company and some were made to accentuate a specific team dynamic in any team. I would have an idea of what was really going on in a team, then I would change the context while maintaining the dynamics. Tossing in a few silly props usually helped to lighten a serious issue.

I must admit that several of the activities are adaptations of other activities. A college professor once told me that the best products come from the second and third generation ideas on a particular theme. I cannot say the adaptations in this book are better than the originals, but they have been very useful in my training and the training conducted by many of my peers.

Why This Stuff Works.

Games and activities are tools. Take a hammer for example, a hammer can be used a multitude of ways such as a paper weight, nail driver, juggler's club, bug killer, screw driver, personal defense, etc. A game or activity is the same way. Its purpose helps to define how you will use it as a tool. You can adapt all the activities in this book to different situations. I encourage trainers to learn what dynamics naturally appear in each of the activities and then start playing with adaptations that work for you. Facilitating variations of an activity encourages you more to closely mirror the true team dynamics and it keeps you from becoming bored.

So let's say that you have picked the right tool for the job. Why do activities work to make teams more effective? I have observed that teams become more effective in two basic areas: tasks (physically getting the job done) and interpersonal skills (how they communicate and treat each other). An activity provides an opportunity for both, but with several advantages over other approaches. Games and initiatives tend to be fun so that people enjoy participating and trying new behaviors. Activities tend to occur within a relatively short span of time so that participants get immediate feedback on performance. The politics and "historical thinking" of situations can be avoided while still recreating the dynamics the team needs to improve. Teams can try several similar activities to gain competency in particular challenge areas. The activities are unique and memorable; people tend to remember what they did and how they did it. Activities are also very flexible. A trainer/facilitator can easily adapt an activity based on such factors as team size, time, resources, personality, and training space.

Role The Facilitator Plays In Making It Happen

Let's look at the term facilitator. A facilitator, in the strictest sense, is a person who makes a process easier. A facilitator does not add or subtract from the substance of a process, but keeps the team focused and moving in a positive direction. An effective facilitator is like a catalyst in a chemical reaction. When certain chemicals are mixed together without a catalyst, the reaction is slow or nonexistent. When the catalyst is added it accelerates a reaction and encourages the formation of a new compound. The interesting note is that the compound neither depletes nor increases the catalyst. The catalyst comes away from the reaction unchanged and can be used again.

The activities alone are fun and engaging, however, a facilitator/trainer has vital roles to play so that the training is more than fun and games. Safety, assessment, sequencing, observation, and debriefing are a few of the important roles.

None of the activities in this book would be enjoyable if the safety of the participants was compromised. I have tried to address the important safety issues especially when they are not obvious. Except in certain cases, I would suggest that the more difficult activities be preceded by simpler games and initiatives so that the team gains confidence and competence as a team before overcoming the "impossible". Stretches before the more active games are also advisable.

When you are observing a team in action, avoid stepping in when they are struggling. Teams need to learn how to handle difficult situations without being rescued by an observer outside the team. Watch for what the team needs to improve, but make a special effort to track what they do well. Often teams that play games and solve fictitious problems learn that their success come from a lack of politics, rank, and "doing things the way we've always done them."

All the roles are important, but the debriefing role is the one that provides the team a link between the activity they just completed and the new behaviors they want to adopt. Ask questions of the team members so that the <u>team</u> reveals the wisdom of what they did and what they learned. Avoid telling them anything. **Consultants tell people what they should do. Facilitators ask open-ended questions so that people can come to their own solutions.** Keep the discussion focused and provide an atmosphere of openness and trust. Facilitate and have fun in the process.

Balloon Castles

Balloon Castles

TIME:
30 min. - 1 hour

PROPS:
Two rolls of transparent tape & 100 balloons for each team of 5-12 people

OBJECTIVE:
Build the tallest free-standing, self-supporting balloon structure possible in 20 minutes.

HISTORY:
As with most of the activities, this one was created from a brainstorm idea Mary Todd and I had prior to working with a team from the Department of Energy. We had divided the team into two sub teams that ultimately joined resources to complete their castle. The tallest castle I have witnessed was over thirteen feet. It was built buy a First of Americas Bank team at the 1994 AQP Conference in Cincinnati, Ohio.

PREPARATION:
Set out 2 rolls of tape in dispensers and count 100 balloons for each team. Be sure to select a space where the ceiling is high enough to accommodate a tall structure.

OBSERVATIONS:
It is really interesting to watch teams plan and do this activity. The **vision** of the finished product is often much different from the actual. Many teams jump right in to the solutions and waste time later trying to define the structure and how to organize it. Some of the most effective teams take a designated time up front to decide a **plan**, make **role assignments**, and come up with one or two **contingencies** before they get busy. Too often teams set lofty goals and forget that a solid foundation is required or the whole thing will tumble to the floor.

Discoveries about balloons and transparent tape are fun to watch. One common strategy is to blow the balloons to full capacity since each one is taller that way. . . until they break! Another common design strategy is to build layers that will fit like a puzzle upon the lower layers. . . too bad the balloons are not a uniform size and shape when they are inflated. The tape causes its own problems since transparent tape can form sharp points that only burst the most critical balloons. The tape can also make one heck of a mess if the participants are not careful where it sticks.

Regardless of what it looks like, every team enjoys a team photo next to their work.

Barbarian Golf

Barbarian Golf

PROPS:
Gather at least one deck tennis ring and orange cone per small group, markers (rope, string, spots, etc.)

SET UP:
Create the golf course by locating different obstacles for the participants to toss the ring through. (For example: over tree limbs, under tables, through fences or holes, across long distances, etc.) Mark the obstacles with a rope. Nine or ten holes is a normal sized course. A course that begins and ends at the same place works well for larger groups so that the teams can start at different holes at the same time.

Divide the team into sub teams of 3-5 people. Give each team at least one cone and one ring. Show the whole group what constitutes a completed shot and let them practice tossing while you show the course to a representative from each of the smaller teams.

INSTRUCTIONS:
Barbarian golf involves tossing a ring and catching it before it hits the ground. Catchers place a cone on their hand (becoming "Cone-Hand the Barbarian") and catch the ring by moving the cone so the ring drops over the cone's point.

A team can have more than one catcher going for the same ring.

Once a catcher catches the ring, the ring must be thrown from the same location (no traveling).

Catches cannot be assisted onto the cone by a free hand, foot, etc.

A thrower can toss the ring in any way to the catcher(s) so long as the ring doesn't hit the ground.

Throwers can be anyone in the team at any time.

Throwers cannot move from their location until the ring is properly caught.

Every forward toss counts as a "stroke". In other words, if a shot is missed by the catcher, the ring goes back to the thrower to be re thrown and each shot toward the catchers is counted as a stroke.

Neither a thrower nor a catcher can be within 5 feet of the hole (obstacle).

Each small team keeps its own score.

Facilitator's note:
Usually par allows for 4-5 strokes per hole.

It's interesting to see if the sub teams compete against each other or cooperate and share best practices.

OFFICIAL SCORE CARD

HOLE #	Strokes	HOLE #	Strokes
1		10	
2		11	
3		12	
4		13	
5		14	
6		15	
7		16	
8		17	**Total**
9		18	

OFFICIAL SCORE CARD

HOLE #	Strokes	HOLE #	Strokes
1		10	
2		11	
3		12	
4		13	
5		14	
6		15	
7		16	
8		17	**Total**
9		18	

Coin Flip, Inc.

Coin Flip, Inc.

TIME:
30 minutes - 1 hour

PROPS:
- 4 quarters
- 2 tape measures
- 2 blank control charts and 1 blank
     histogram chart
- Markers
- Masking tape
- 2 calculators

OBJECTIVE:
To teach participants how to gather and chart data for an X-bar/R control chart and histogram. Participants flip coins trying to land them as close to a line of tape as possible.

HISTORY:
I created this activity to help explain the important aspects of collecting data and how the same data can be used in several ways. I use the coin flip in my Successful Tools and Techniques Seminar (STATS) with much success. Who would have thought you could teach even therapists to use control charts?

PREPARATION:
This activity can be challenging for facilitators that are unfamiliar with histograms and control charts. I would suggest learning what you can before presenting this activity.

Place a six-foot strip of masking tape on the floor eight feet from and parallel to an unobstructed wall. This will mark the tossing line for the activity. Place another six-foot strip of masking tape on the floor eighteen inches from and parallel to the same wall. This will mark the goal line for the activity.

Prepare a flip chart sheet for a run chart and another for a histogram. Participants can use the templates provided for the initial records then move the information to the larger charts so that everyone can see.

SCENARIO:

You are employees of Coin Flip, Incorporated (CFI). CFI has been establish for three generations and has had the best reputation for placing the currency of its customers.

The money placement industry is a little known spin-off of the stock market. Money is given to CFI to literally flip toward a target. Based on the flip, customers either receive a certain level of return or loss on their investment. The founder of CFI created this brilliantly designed business while traveling through Nevada.

Your jobs are to take two coins and flip each of them so that they land as near as you can place them to the tape near the wall. As everyone knows in the money placement business, you are not allowed to cross the starting line during the toss and the toss must arc more than head high before landing.

Tracking performance is very important at CFI. All flips must be measured and rounded to the nearest inch.

The business looks carefully at your overall performance to consider pay increases and employment. The business tries to break even (average placements equal zero) to avoid taxes. However, each negative placement is money that the customer loses. If the customer loses his money, he spreads negative publicity. If he spreads negative publicity, we lose customers. If we lose customers, eventually CFI goes bankrupt.

INSTRUCTIONS:

Ask the team to develop a process for who measures the distance each coin lands from the strip of tape near the wall. This inspector measures the distance from the masking tape to the location where the coin stops.

For the Average and Range charts make sure a team member writes down the distance each time a coin is flipped and figures the average (plot the average on the graph) and range of the 2 consecutive flips each person makes. Upper and lower control limits will be added to the graph after all the tosses.

At the same time, data for the histogram should be gathered from each shot and later graphed. This is done by simply recording every toss' distance on the histogram template.

Each coin must flip above the flipper's head before the coin lands. This rule helps make the variance greater and the process change more dramatic if you attempt the activity's variation written below.

Everyone shoots, taking turns, until at least 40 shots have been made (Allow everyone to practice first). The starting line is 8 feet from the wall. Ask them to chart the distance each coin lands from the center of the tape.

FACILITATOR NOTES:

The team calculates averages by adding the distances that both coins land from the tape, then divide by two.

For example: 4" + -11" = -7   -7/2= -3.5"

The team calculates the ranges by subtracting the smallest number from the largest. A range value is an absolute number so it is always positive.

For example: 4" - -11" = 15"

To calculate the upper control limits (UCL) and lower control limits (LCL) for the average chart you first will need to average all the averages and average all the ranges. Use the following formula to determine the control limits:

UCLx = average of the averages + (1.88 X
average of the ranges)
LCLx = average of the averages - (1.88 X
average of the ranges)

To calculate the upper control limits (UCL) and lower control limits (LCL) for the range chart you will need to use the following formula:

UCL_R = 3.27 X average of the ranges

LCL_R = 0

The formulas above are only good for X-bar & R chart that has a sample size of two (in this case two flips per person each time). If you need the formulas for larger sample sizes, refer to a statistic book or SPC manual.

Variation:
After trying the activity as it is written above, ask the group to feel free to change the work process the best way they can to meet their customer's needs. Have groups come up with the best solutions, shoot 20 times and chart the results.

Turn charts into control charts with upper and lower control limits based on their shots. Explain control charts and histograms and compare their beginning performance to their last.

Coin Flip Sample Chart and Set-up

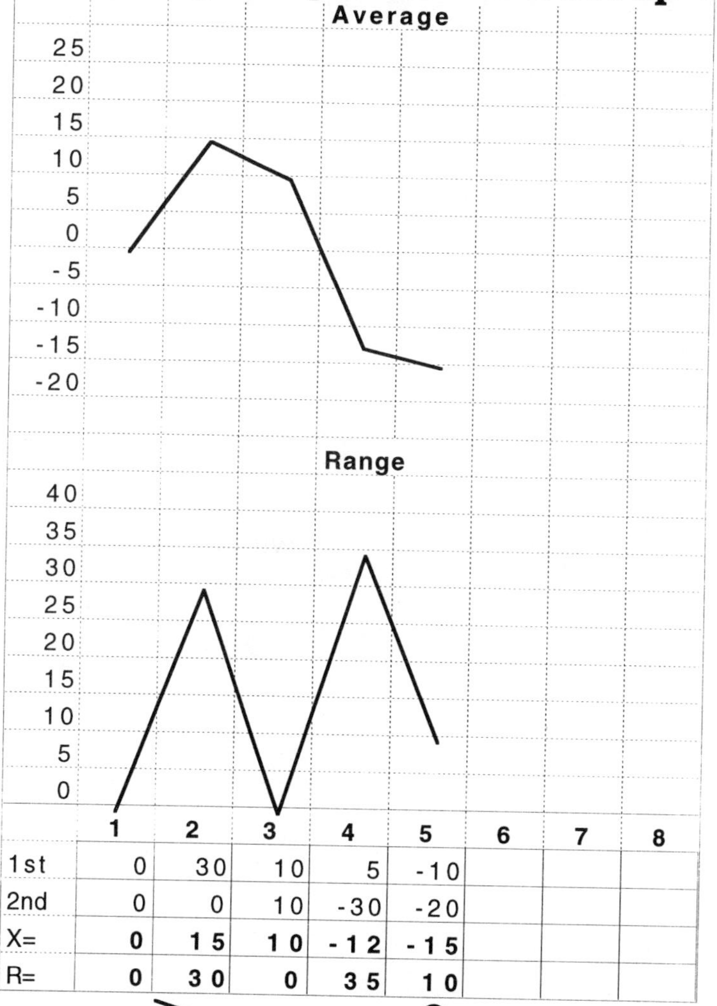

Average

Range

	1	2	3	4	5	6	7	8
1st	0	30	10	5	-10			
2nd	0	0	10	-30	-20			
X=	0	15	10	-12	-15			
R=	0	30	0	35	10			

Average

	1	2	3	4	5	6	7	8	9
60									
56									
52									
48									
44									
40									
36									
32									
28									
24									
20									
16									
12									
8									
4									
0									
-4									
-8									
average -12									
inches -16									

Range

	1	2	3	4	5	6	7	8	9
56									
52									
48									
44									
40									
36									
32									
28									
24									
20									
16									
12									
8									
4									
0									
	1	**2**	**3**	**4**	**5**	**6**	**7**	**8**	**9**
Shot 1									
Shot 2									
X=									
R=									

					Average				60
									56
									52
									48
									44
									40
									36
									32
									28
									24
									20
									16
									12
									8
									4
									0
									-4
									-8
									-12
									-16
					Range				
									56
									52
									48
									44
									40
									36
									32
									28
									24
									20
									16
									12
									8
									4
									0
10	11	12	13	14	15	16	18	19	20

Histogram

	-40 to -36	-35 to -31	-30 to -26	-25 to -21	-20 to -16	-15 to -11	-10 to -6	-5 to -1	0 to 4	5 to 9	10 to 14	15 to 18
30												
29												
28												
27												
26												
25												
24												
23												
22												
21												
20												
19												
18												
17												
16												
15												
14												
13												
12												
11												
10												
9												
8												
7												
6												
5												
4												
3												
2												
1												

Compass Walk

Compass Walk

OBJECTIVE:
Present the group with two experiential examples of independent versus team performance.
First time -- individuals try to find a spot by themselves on the ground while blind, mute.
Second time -- the team tries to find the spot while blind.

PROPS:
Orange cone, one poly spot, blindfolds

PREPARATION:
Place spot with cone on top of it approximately 30 yards from where the group will start their journey.

INSTRUCTIONS:
Everyone needs to line up along the starting line so that they can see the cone across the field. You will be trying to find the spot that is under the cone. A facilitator will remove the cone from the spot after everyone is blindfolded, but the spot will not be moved.

On your individual journey you must go blindly, silently, alone and with your hands in front of you so that you won't bump into anyone or anything. The facilitators will be spotting for you so you don't walk off a cliff or anything, but there are so many of you compared to us, we may yell "Stop"! Stop means you just freeze where you are and wait until you hear "Go!" or get informed of some hazard that may lie ahead of you.

As soon as you feel as if you are as close to the spot as you think you will get (without necessarily touching it), take off your blindfold, and remain silent until everyone has stopped. THIS IS NOT A RACE.

(Once everyone has traveled and stopped.)

Take a look around. . . see where you are and where everyone else is in relation to the goal. Let's gather around the spot to talk about your strategies.

(After the debrief, give the team 4 minutes to come up with a plan for doing the activity again.)

This time blindness will be your only restriction. The starting place will be the same and the goal will remain where it was before.

FACILITATOR NOTE:

The team searches for the goal the second time and usually finds the spot after a few minutes. Most solutions involve` the whole team lining up and holding hands to "sweep" the ground for the spot.

If the team does not find the goal on the second round, you can ask them to try again after another planning session or stop to discuss what is keeping them from reaching their goal.

Don't Touch Me !!!

Don't Touch Me ! ! !

TIME:
30 minutes to 1 hour with processing

OBJECTIVE:
The object of this game is for everyone to touch the object in the middle and switch places with his partner as fast as possible without touching anyone. Common Issues: Shifting Paradigms, Brainstorming, Continuous Improvement, Integrity, Cooperation, Coordination, Communication, Benchmarking

PROPS:
• An eight inch spot for 6-16 people, or a cone for 18-26 people, or a hula-hoop for larger groups, • Stopwatch

HISTORY:
I got this activity from Karl Rohnke's Bag of Tricks publication #50, page 514. I detailed the instructions some more and tried it out on an unsuspecting corporate group that was working to "think outside the box." It was a hit and has been a classic activity for several facilitators I have trained.

PREPARATION:
Locate an open area large enough for a loose circle of players. Be sure you have at least six players.

Place your spot, cone, or hoop on the ground in the center of the circle of people.

INSTRUCTIONS:
Pick a partner from across the circle. Each person should have his own partner.

The object of this game is for everyone to touch the spot and switch places with their partner as quickly as possible without touching anyone in the process.

While you are in motion, say "Don't touch me!" like you mean it until you have reached your partner's position.

I will be timing the group for the overall time it takes the group to accomplish the task. Each time someone touches someone else, one second is added to the group's overall time.

As soon as someone says "START!" and the group starts, I will begin the time and then stop the clock when everyone has reached his or her new position and someone has said "STOP!".

So the rules are that everyone has to touch the spot, switch places with your partner while saying "Don't touch me!" because each time someone is touched it adds a second to the group's overall time.

What questions do you have?

FACILITATOR'S NOTES:

This activity requires an even number of participants. If your group is uneven, add or subtract yourself to even it up.

Questions from the group usually come from everyone eventually. Answer their questions by restating the parameters of the task. "The rules are that everyone has to touch the spot, switch places with their partner while saying "Don't touch me!" because each time someone is touched it adds a second to the group's overall time."

Let the group try to decrease their time until they are satisfied. If their best time is fairly long (6-10 seconds), gently state a shorter time achieved by a previous group and see if they want to try again. A benchmark of 1.45 seconds is a good time.

A common process groups go through in getting from a 12-15 second process to a 1.45 second process involves a few distinct discoveries. 1) Move closer to the spot. 2) We can move the spot. 3) Work smarter, not harder. 4) You can stand next to your partner. 5)

How do we define "changing places with your partner"?

There is one potential problem with this activity. It is a "eureka" problem (It has a limited number of final solutions.) If someone in your group has played it before, he or she might diminish the effect of the activity by jumping in with a final solution.

Easy. . . Knot!

Easy. . . Knot!

PROPS:
• A ten foot rope
• A 30-50 foot rope which is a different type from the 10 foot rope

OBJECTIVE:
Large team ties an overhand knot at the secured end of a long rope without touching the secured end.

HISTORY:
This activity was created for a group of forty people who wanted a quick activity to include new members into their team. They had done experiential activities previously and wanted the new members to try a rope puzzle. In this team's case, each person had a carabiner that they attached over the rope. About fifteen minutes later they had their knot! In other groups, this activity has taken as long as an hour.

PREPARATION:
Tie the two ropes securely together to make a longer rope.

Tie the other end of the shorter rope to a stationary object such as a column, doorway, or post.

INSTRUCTIONS:
Start the activity asking, "How many people know how to tie a simple overhand knot?" It is the first knot you tie when you tie your shoe laces. You might have to demonstrate an overhand knot with the rope.

Ask everyone in the group to line up and grab the long rope with one hand. No one should be holding the shorter rope that is attached to the longer rope and secured at the end.

The goal of the group is to tie a simple overhand knot in the short rope without touching the short rope in the process. The facilitator should be able to easily identify the knot when you are done.

Constraints:
* Everyone can slide along the long rope, but cannot let go of it or trade places with anyone in the line.

* The short rope cannot be touched.

* The long and short ropes cannot be untied.

One solution strategy:
The whole team should slide toward the loose end of the long rope to create some unoccupied space on the long rope. The person closest to the short and long rope connection forms a loop in the excess long rope and steps through the loop. The rest of the group will also have to step through the loop just like the first person. When everyone is through, the team should have a loosely tied overhand knot. The team can maneuver the loose knot toward the short rope and pull it tight in the short rope with a little work. Most teams seem to send the person at the loose end of the long rope around the group to form the knot. That strategy will work, but it may be more confusing.

Feeding the Zircon Gorilla

Feeding the Zircon Gorilla

INTRODUCTION:
This activity was developed specifically to address the issues of accounting and inventory. Twenty-nine store managers were being trained during a week long session and this activity was supposed to offer them an opportunity to practice some of their new skills. To make it "realistic" we added quite a lot of complexity. Customer/supplier issues, work flow, honesty, competition versus cooperation all played major roles within the activity. Don't try this one alone. There are so many things to prepare and attend to that it could get too confusing for one facilitator.

OBJECTIVE:
Starting with a central supplier, sell goods to customers and account for your volume of sales.

HISTORY:
QuikTrip Corporation, one of the customers that uses our services, asked us to create an activity that would address some inventory issues and get everyone at their management development conference involved. I roughed out the scenario and logistics then turned the idea over to the in-house trainers. They liked the activity, but thought it needed some ridiculous extras to make it fun. We added knee-highs, latex feet, and some swim gear. The resulting video increased in value by the minute.

Facilitator Information

How the game works
Central Supply must go to its vendor, the facilitators, (and pay them with a "sincere complement") to fill the 3 gallon bucket with water. The bucket of water is dumped into Central Supply's 40 gallon container from which Store cups are filled. Central Supply provides the Stores large cups and the special

container (baster) to fill the customer's cups. The Store pays Central Supply a handshake while holding the full cup. Central Supply is responsible for its record keeping. Central Supply personnel filling the 40 gallon container must wear swim fins, goggles, and a snorkel. Those filling Store cups must wear swim goggles (covered so they can't see out of one eye).

Stores purchase large cups of water from Central Supply with a handshake (while holding the full cup). The cup must be emptied into the store's 1-gallon bucket. The store sells water to customers when the customers give a praise (customer contact). The store must use the baster to fill the cup. (Baster and small cups provided by Central Supply.) Stores must keep record of purchases and sales.

Customers are given their first small cup when they buy a cup of water with a "customer contact". Customers must buy one cup of water from each store. They can then select the stores from which to purchase up to 2 more cups of water (per store) based on the service they receive. Customers empty their purchases into the space ship's holding tank (40 gallon container). Customers must keep record of purchases.

Supplies
(may need more or less if 5 stores not used)
- Two of the same size large containers (approximately 40 gallons)
- Two 3-gallon buckets (to fill Central Supply)
- Five 1-gallon buckets (for stores)
- One sleeve large Styrofoam cups (for stores to get from Central Supply)
- One sleeve small Styrofoam cups (for customers)
- A water supply
- One dozen pens
- Five store markers (hula hoops)
- Instructions and forms for Supply. Stores, and Customers
- Video camera and tape
- Five meat basters
- Big feet

- Headgear (tennis balls in X-large knee-high stockings)
- Swim goggles, flippers, snorkels

Organization (will change based on number of participants)
- Central Supply: 4 people
- Stores: 2 people per store (10)
- Customers: 3 people (aliens) per store (15)

Observers
- Analyze forms for winning store
- Measure remaining amounts of water in buckets

Facilitators
- Debrief each group separately (Note: Observers can form their own group.)
- Gather groups together and have representative from each group summarize their group's discussion
- Ask whole group for overall process improvements related to real inventory situations, DiSC, Situational Leadership, etc.

Top View of Layout

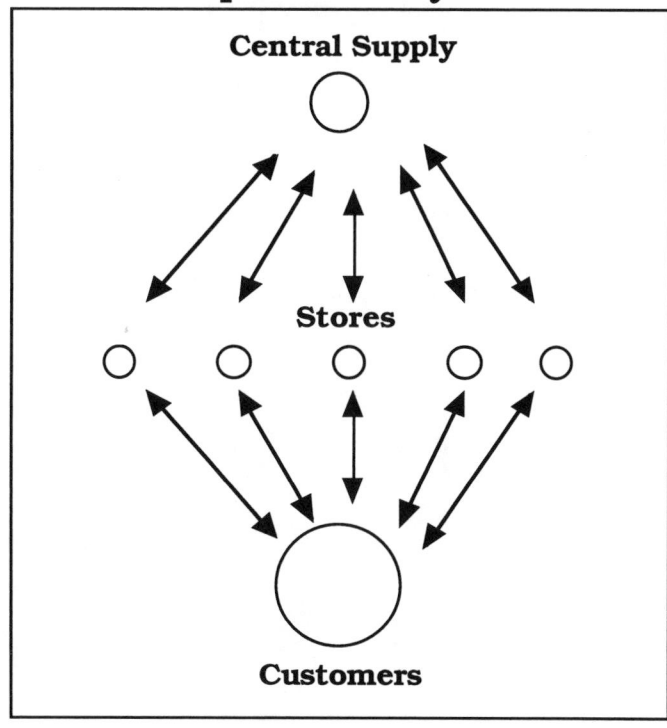

CENTRAL ACCOUNTING
INVENTORY CONTROL FORM

	WATER VOLUME			
	PURCHASED	SOLD	REMAINING INVENTORY	+/- INVENTORY
CENTRAL SUPPLY				
STORES				
Store 1				
Store 2				
Store 3				
Store 4				
Store 5				
TOTAL				
ZIRCON SOLAR SYSTEM				
Planet 1				
Planet 2				
Planet 3				
Planet 4				
Planet 5				
TOTAL				

Customers

• You are part of a team of aliens from the solar system Zircon. Your group represents each one of the five inhabited planets in the Zircon system (Tex, Am, Tenn, Sun, and Con). You are on a top secret mission to collect a special liquid from the planet Earth that is needed on your planet. The Earthlings do not suspect that the liquid they sell is so precious.

Each of the Zircon planets has herds of gorillas that feed on a small weasel-like animal called "Akos". The name of each of the Zircon planets is the prefix for each species. The gorillas must have this special liquid in order to wash down the "Akos" as they eat them.

• You must carefully gather the liquid so that none of it is spilled.

• You must wear a special headgear to make sure the Earth's sunlight doesn't effect your brain or cause your hair to fall into this precious liquid.

• So the Earthlings do not suspect your diabolic plan, each member of your team must visit every store 1 time in random order (plan it out). After gathering the first mandatory cup, you can gather another 2 cups from those stores that give you exceptional service. (No more than 3 cups per store maximum.) Don't let the Earthlings suspect or see any plan.

• The Earthlings will "sell" you the fuel for a bit of "positive feedback". Carefully and quickly take a full cup to the fuel tank for your planet, empty the cup into the central tank of your space ship before returning to the next store. Millions on your planet are awaiting your homecoming. Good luck!

• You will need to complete the attached expense account form so you can be reimbursed when you get back to your planet. Have it ready before takeoff.

• When you have memorized this message, eat it. . . not.

ZIRCON EXPENSE REPORT FORM

Planet: _____

Purchased from Store Number	Number of Fuel Containers Purchased
1	
2	
3	
4	
5	
TOTAL CONTAINERS PURCHASED	
Total number containers purchased times volume of containers	
TOTAL VOLUME PURCHASED	

Stores

• Your store is desperately struggling to be the best store in the division.

• Central Supply has been fortunate to accumulate a fairly large supply of water during the recent world-wide drought.

• Because water is scarce, a central supply station is available so you can replenish your store's supply by ordering it and picking it up from the suppliers. The cost to purchase each unit of water is a handshake that must be given while holding the full cup. You will be provided with the cup on your first visit to Central Supply. You must wear the special protective footgear provided by the company on your trips to and from Central Supply.

• The drought has left many foreigners without water, so you can expect booming water sales from strange looking and speaking individuals seeking cups of water. (Remember what makes this company a quality-minded business.) Your customers will pay you for the cup of water with positive feedback. The price is one positive feedback per cup.

• Customers can only be served from your store's bucket using the special dispenser provided for you.

• Attached is the form used to track inventory and sales. Complete it as purchases and sales are made and be prepared to hand over the completed form shortly after the shift is complete.

STORE INVENTORY CONTROL FORM

PURCHASES # of Containers Purchased		SALES # of Cups Sold	
TOTAL CONTAINERS PURCHASED		**TOTAL NUMBER OF CUPS SOLD**	
TOTAL VOLUME PURCHASED		**TOTAL VOLUME OF CUPS SOLD**	
Remaining Inventory			
Total volume purchased less volume sold and inventory			

Central Supply

• You are the central suppliers of water to the stores. Fortunately for you a drought has caused a world-wide shortage of water and the price of water has skyrocketed.

• You must pay your supplier a sincere compliment for each container of water you purchase. Because of the hazards of securing the water you must wear the appropriate protective gear when purchasing the water.

• You should charge your customers (the stores) 1 handshake per cup for the water (given while the full cup is being held by the store buyer).

• Unfortunately the demand for your limited supply is so great that you have to carefully control how much each store can buy at a time. (A store can only buy what it can carry away in a large cup.)

• Track the water sales on the attached form and be prepared to hand over the completed form shortly after the sales run.

CENTRAL SUPPLY

CONTAINERS PURCHASED FROM OUTSIDE VENDORS	SALES		
	STORE #	CONTAINERS OF WATER SOLD	TOTAL
	1		
	2		
	3		
	4		
	5		
Total Volume of Containers Purchased			
Minus Total Volume of Containers Sold			
Calculated Total Remaining Inventory (Volume)			
Actual Total Remaining Inventory (Volume)			

Fing Fong Fooey

Fing Fong Fooey

OBJECTIVE:
This activity creates a way for a group to decide who will do or get something.

HISTORY:
A friend of mine, Kathi Burns, taught me this tie breaker. It's great. She explained that she would use this decision making activity to determine who got the last cookie or who had to wash the dishes. I like it because it uses random selection that is rarely predictable.

INSTRUCTIONS:
The activity starts off like the Rock, Paper, Scissors game except that each person will hold out 1, 2, or 3 fingers after the count.

With everyone in a circle, count off (fists striking open hands) "fing, fong, fooey" and end with everyone's fingers pointing showing their choice of 1, 2, or 3.

Add the number of fingers exposed.

Then, starting with yourself, count each person around the circle until you reach the total number fingers counted.

The last person counted is "it".

For example: You have five people in a group and all together you say "fing, fong, fooey". Add the number of fingers showing (let's say it's 10) then count each person around the circle until you reach 10. In this case, the person right next to you is "it".

If you have multiple people to select, just predetermine something like, "The chosen people will be the 4 people to the right of 'it'."

Giant Texas Lizard Egg

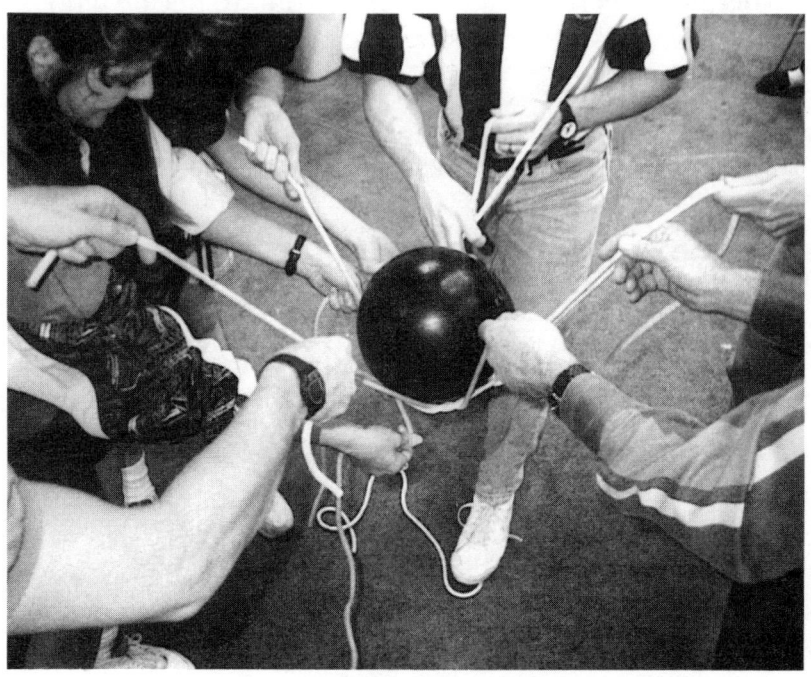

Giant Texas Lizard Egg

TIME:
30 min. - 1 hour

PROPS:
1 bowling ball, at least one 3 to 6 foot rope per participant, a milk crate or canvass bag

OBJECTIVE:
Move a bowling ball across the floor and into a basket using ropes.

HISTORY:
I thought-up this activity while riding in the back of a car. I had never seen a bowling ball used in any initiatives, yet every other type of ball seemed to be used. I found a great 16 pound ball at a local thrift store for $1.45 and I was ready to go. The whole idea of a giant Texas lizard egg came from Steve Balsters, a good friend and mentor. His scenario for the Giant Texas Lizard (tire on pole) event has always made challenge course participants ask, "Is this true?"

SCENARIO:
You have found yourselves in the middle of a crisis. An egg from a giant Texas lizard has rolled from its nest and needs to be replaced before the mother returns. Unfortunately, the shell of the lizard egg has properties of the adult lizard's tail; it emits a sweet odor but is highly toxic. Fortunately for you, a game warden has left some specially treated ropes nearby for just such an incident. The ropes have been treated with radiation to eliminate the possibility of a premature hatching. The radiation is at tolerable levels, however, over-exposure causes instant and terrible side effects such as blindness, muteness, or confusion. I once saw several team members develop a "death grip" on each of their ropes when they were over-exposed. Over-exposure occurs when a person touches his own rope with more than one hand. Somehow you must discover a way to move the egg, without breaking it, back into its nest before the mother returns. Be sure not to contact the egg with anything but the treated ropes. Don't over-expose

yourselves. . . and don't even try moving that nest. Giant Texas lizards are especially sensitive to movement of their nests. I understand the mother lizards grow to 300 pounds and can strike faster than a snake when they are protecting their young. Good luck!

The Great Nail Puzzle

The Great Nail Puzzle

Once upon a time, in a rainy country, there was a great competition between two ancient groups of builders, the Assentites and the Pancakians. Each group believed that they had the single best way to construct a building. The Assentites believed that all buildings should be constructed upon a single room and extend high beyond the clouds so that no roof was necessary to keep out the rain. The Pancakians believed that every building should be made of many rooms and the top of the building should reach no higher than ten feet and have a flat roof. Both construction methods had problems. The tall buildings required enormous amounts of building materials and years of hard labor. The short flat-roofed buildings often leaked from the rain and drowned the residents. The battle between the groups of constructors raged until the land and people suffered greatly. Finally, a white-haired wise man attempted to solve the conflict for the good of everyone. He presented a puzzle to both sides so they might see the error in their rigid ways. He said, "Here are 16 nails and a small block of wood with a single nail embedded into it. Using only these materials, balance all sixteen nails upon the head of the single

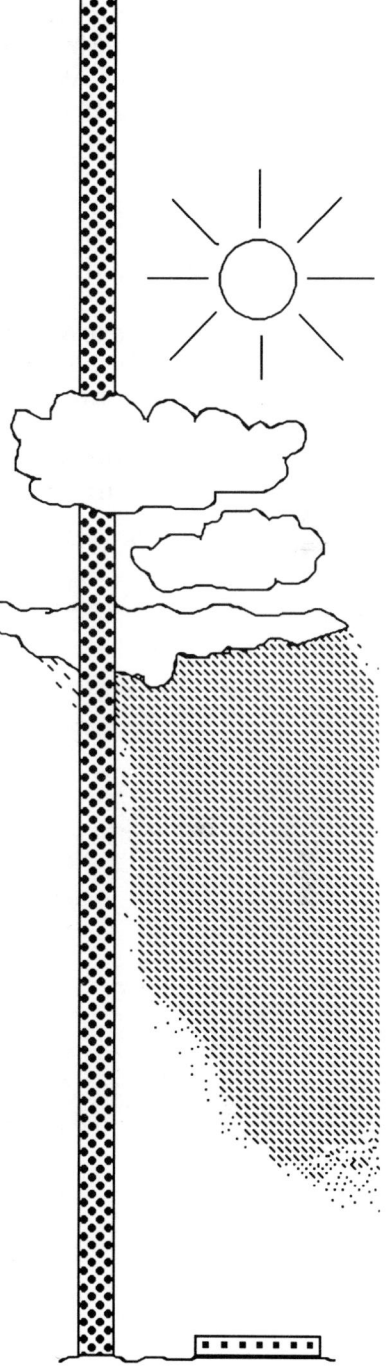

nail. Surely, the person or group who can solve this puzzle will be worthy enough to design all our future buildings." With the wise man's words in mind, all of the builders tried and tried to find the solution. Days then weeks passed but not one of the builders succeeded. Everyone was about to give up on the puzzle when a man from the distant country of Zipperon passed the territory for the first time. He heard the groans of the builders and offered to help. After a few minutes of thought, he showed the builders the solution. The amazed builders said in unison, "OF COURSE !" when they saw the nails and gave the man a great party. This outsider had solved the puzzle, saved many people from drowning, conserved the natural resources, and changed construction methods forever. Solve the puzzle and discover how this man changed history.

The Grid

The Grid

PROPS:
A grid approximately 8 X 12 feet. (You can make one by taping a grid onto a tarp with masking tape or just use a premade grid found on a tile floor or as a pattern on carpeting.) Get 9-12 coins or other appropriate objects to represent the team's resources. Use copies of the maps provided to track the group's progress.

OBJECTIVE:
The object of this activity is to get your whole team to the other end of the grid by discovering the set path through the grid.

PREPARATION:
Choose your map and get a pen to mark the incorrect steps. I have found that it is best to put a line through the square each time a person steps on an incorrect square and then another when the square is stepped on again. Put the grid on the floor and divide the group in half for a two-way grid or in thirds for the three-way grid.

INSTRUCTIONS:
There are many ways to facilitate this activity. The following are the instructions for the one-way grid, two-way grid, and three-way grid. One of these three may "fit" best for your team depending on your needed emphasis.

One-way Grid
The team may only send one person at a time to discover the path from one end of the grid to the other. As you discover the correct path, any adjacent square may be tried. If you tried jumping rows, you might never successfully discover the path.

The facilitator will be able to give your team verbal information limited to whether the squares you have chosen are on the path or not. If you choose a square off the path, you must follow the correct path back to the start and someone else on your team must be sent out to try again.

A correct square is always correct and an incorrect square is always incorrect.

Each time you step in an incorrect square a second time or more, the team loses one of its resources. If you take risks and choose incorrectly, a start-over is required. If you take a risk and choose a wrong square that has already been explored it is rework and will cost the team one resource.

The team may coach the person moving through the grid from any position outside the grid. You cannot mark the trail in any way and no physical maps may be constructed. Once the team has started, any square touched by anyone counts as a try even if it is by accident.

If the resources are eliminated, terrible consequences will result. . . debt? There can be a way for a team to recover its losses after the path has been discovered. The team's leader must be blindfolded and guided alone through the grid without stepping off the path.

Emphasis: Problem solving, communication, decision making

Two-Way Grid
Each small team may only send one person at a time to discover the path. The teams start at opposite ends of the grid. Both teams are part of the same organization.

The parameters are the same as the one-way grid except that two people may be on the grid at the same time -- one from each end.

Facilitator Notes:
• Tracking the participant's progress is easier if two facilitators work off the same map and each one watches a team.

• Divide the resources between the teams. Eight to twelve resources work best.
• Participants often ask if the path is really continuous or, if both teams are on the same path. I usually reply that it is a "process of discovery".
• The two teams are still part of the same organization so a wrong square tried by one team counts for the second time if the other team touches it and a resource is lost.

Emphasis: Cooperation versus competition, problem solving, sharing resources, blending departments, communication, trust

Three-Way Grid
Each small team may only send one person at a time to discover the path. The teams start at the wide side of the grid. All of the teams are part of the same organization.

The parameters are the same as the one-way grid except that three people may be on the grid at the same time -- one from each team.

Facilitator Notes:
• Tracking the participant's progress is easier if three facilitators work off the same map and each one watches a team. There are three entrances on the three-way grid -- each team must start from a different place. Some confusion occurs with some teams until each team discovers the beginning of its path. You might explain that each small team comes at a problem from a different perspective but a common goal.
• Divide the resources among the teams. Twelve resources work best.
• Participants often ask if the path is continuous or, if all of the teams have different paths. I reply that it is a "process of discovery".
• The three teams are still part of the same organization so a wrong square tried by one team counts for the second time if the another team touches it and a resource is lost. If the resources from one small team are depleted and another

resource is lost, the additional resource comes from one of the other two teams. They are all working from the same budget.

Emphasis: Cooperation versus competition, problem solving, sharing resources, coordination, blending departments, communication, trust, leadership, conflict

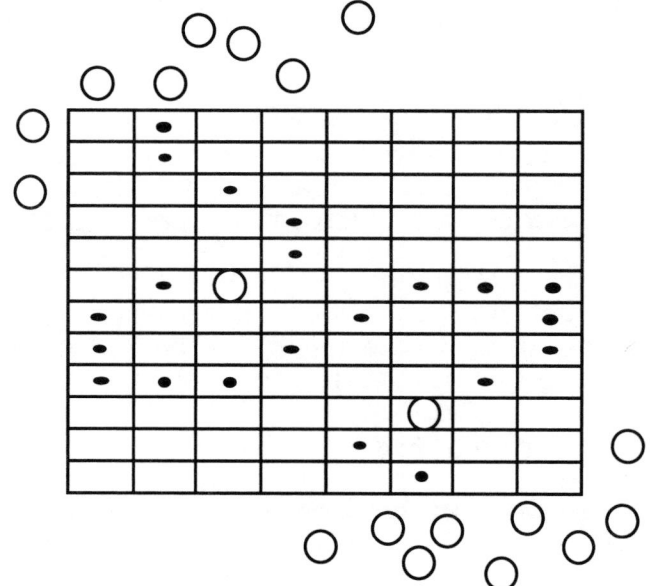

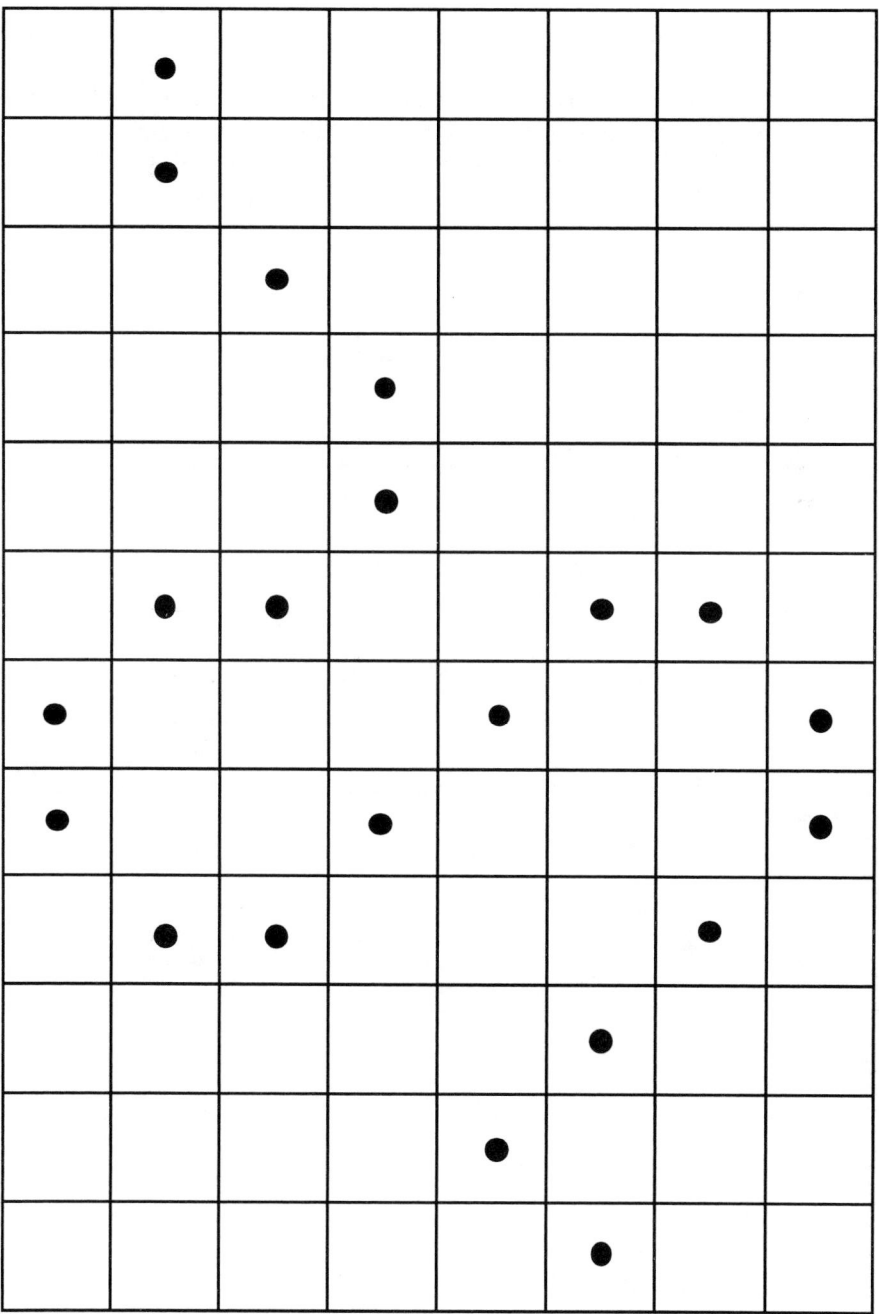

One- or Two-Way Grid

Three-Way Grid

The Group Leader

The Group Leader

PROPS:
- Stick or pipe long enough to accommodate a team of participants
- Bandannas
- Bucket of water with a handle
- Hula hoop or small circle of rope

OBJECTIVE:
Team of blindfolded participants, with the vision of their leader, tries to hang a bucket of water on a hook (branch) without spilling any water.

HISTORY:
I created this activity with the word "empowerment" in mind. The idea was to let the group select at least one leader to give them "vision" while the rest did their jobs. Would the leader assume the team had no say in the process and maintain control (micro-manage) or would the leader solicit input of ideas and improvement opportunities, etc.?

The group leader went from hypothetical to reality in a workshop at the 1994 Challenge Course Practitioners Symposium. It went exceptionally well.

PREPARATION:
Find a location outside with several trees. One tree needs a hook (branch) on which the blind participants can easily hang the water bucket.

Fill the bucket with water to within one inch of the top and place it approximately one foot from the hoop and between the leader and the team's destination. (The blinded team will probably lift the bucket with the end of the pipe and have to rotate 180 degrees before heading to the hook.)

Place the hoop approximately 25 feet away from the hook. For added challenge, position the hoop so that the sighted leader will have difficulty seeing the bucket when the team is about to hang it.

INSTRUCTIONS:

The next activity has a leadership role(s) and worker roles. Ask the team to select a leader or a set of leaders.

The leader(s) should stand in the hoop where you placed it earlier. The hoop cannot be moved and the leader(s) must stay inside it.

Team members should blindfold themselves and take their places at the pipe. Team members must maintain contact (both hands) with the pipe at all times. No one can touch the water or the bucket.

The team leader(s) gives the team coaching. If water is spilled and disaster strikes, the whole team can start over (miraculous regeneration).

If you have additional people, they can become the "voices of competition". The voices can say anything that a business competitor might say, but the volume should be kept to a whisper. People whispering as the competition cannot physically hinder the team's progress.

Indoors Variation:

A bucket can be hung upside down from the end of a pipe or broom handle and be used to cover something on the floor like a magic marker. Of course there are terrible consequences for knocking over the marker.

Position the marker upright almost in the corner of the room. Place the hoop in the opposite corner of the room.

Gutterball

Gutterball

PROPS:
* Inexpensive quarter-round sticks (the wooden or plastic trim sticks that are used to cover the edges of wall corners) Any hardware store will have a selection. Buy the cheapest kind in the store. I have found that the simulated wood is best because it bends instead of breaking. **Beware of leaving the plastic gutters in a hot vehicle, they tend to deform with the heat.**

* A steel ball, marble, or ball of hard candy

* A stop watch

OBJECTIVE:
Roll a ball from person to person as quickly as possible without dropping it.

HISTORY:
To tell the truth, I cannot remember if I created this activity or not. Who knows? Who cares? It has been an effective tool for training creativity and problem solving. The first time I taught other facilitators how to do the activity was at the 1993 OTRA conference at Cross Point Camp in Oklahoma. Gutterball had been a successful activity with several teams before it "went public".

INSTRUCTIONS:
Ask everyone to stand in a circle, then give each person a gutter or ask people to pair up and give each pair one gutter. The gutter per person method is great, but if you want to focus on partnership or don't have enough gutters, use the pair method.

Use the gutters you have to transport this ball from the first person to the next all the way around and then back to the first person.

Now that you have a feel for the task, lets try for an efficient and effective process. Try to send the ball through the process as fast as you can, beginning and ending on the first person's gutter. This time there will be a few constraints for solving the problem.

　　　＊ No one's gutter can be skipped.

　　　＊ Gutters cannot touch each other.

　　　＊ Gutter per person method - Your own pinkies must be touching each other all the time.

　　　＊ Gutter per pair method - Each person must choose one end of the gutter to hold and hold it within three inches of the end.

　　　＊ People cannot touch the ball as it travels from beginning, through the process and back to the beginning.

　　　＊ If the ball falls from a gutter, the process must be restarted.

SCENARIO:

Your team has been commissioned to help a candy factory with their production process. The company has observed from its place in the market that its cycle time is too long. Candy is taking too long to go from the first conveyor in the plant, around the to each of the stations and back to the beginning of the production cycle.

Your task as a consultant team is to first replicate their current process (pass the ball all the way around) and then discover ways to decrease cycle time without reducing the number of steps (gutters) in the process.

FACILITATOR NOTES:

The solution for gutterball is similar to warp speed that asks a team to juggle a ball as quickly around the group as possible. The gutters seem to add an extra challenge and paradigm shift to the final solution.

If you are working with kids, be aware of possible "sword" fights which commonly occur with the gutters. Potential for injury increases with each new weapon.

Most teams of ten to fifteen people tend to get their time down to seven or eight seconds before benchmarking a "world record". A "world record" time tends to be under one second! If it seems impossible, good. . . but it can be done.

I have witnessed a wide variety of record breaking techniques. A C.A.T. team from Ford currently holds the fastest time I have witnessed at .21 seconds! The variety of possible strategies and solutions is a strength of this activity.

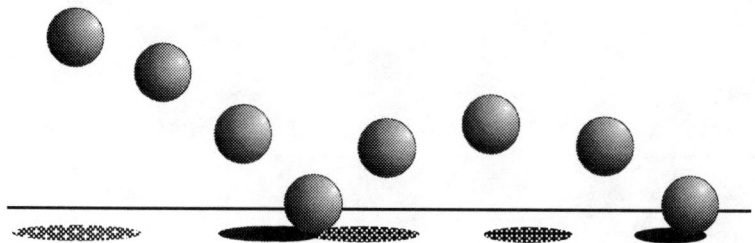

Horizontal Spider Web

Horizontal Spider Web

PROPS:
A pre-made spider's web or some string to make one, something to tie the web to such as two folding tables, bells or some alarm system

OBJECTIVE:
Move the team from one side of the web to the other by going through the web (from underneath, out the top) without touching it.

HISTORY:
I heard this great twist on an old favorite from the staff at Camp Lutherhoma near Tahlequah, Oklahoma. I tried it on some willing peers and it worked very well.

PREPARATION:
Tie the web approximately 2 1/2 feet from the ground. It should be strung horizontally. Be sure the tables, or to whatever you tie the web, are secured so that they will not fall on the participants if the web is pulled.

Place bells or other alarms strategically on the web so that participants can tell if they disturb the web.

SCENARIO:
You are all part of a special team, chosen for its effectiveness. You have been asked to find information in a competitor's computer system to set benchmarks for your own company. You have successfully avoided the elaborate security system and gathered the information you need. Now you have to get out before the security officers make their rounds. Unfortunately, one obstacle remains between you and freedom.

A high tech alarm system has been activated that will seal off the building and alert authorities if its laser beams or force fields are disturbed. A reset switch has been placed under the flooring on your side of the system that can be activated by the weight of everyone on your team standing the floor on that side. (In other words, if the alarm is rung, everyone has to start over from the beginning.) The gaps in the laser network seal off each time a body passes through a hole. A force field exists on the far side of the system between the floor and the edge. Another one foot high strip exists between the ceiling and the edge on the near side.

Work carefully and safely and you may make it out free and with those huge bonuses you were promised.

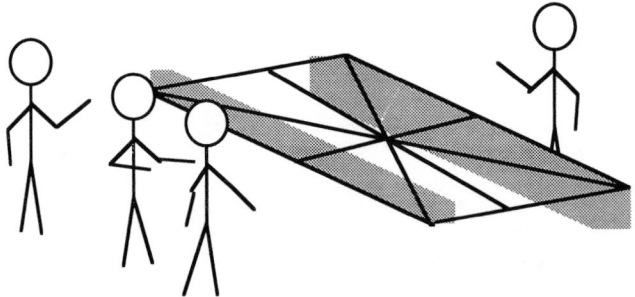

OBSERVATIONS:

The frequency at which the traditional spider web has been facilitated to teams has made this small change in set-up key to keeping the activity fresh. The traditional web has a well-defined strategy for completion. People look at the horizontal web and assume a similar strategy, but the solution is quite different.

Humans do not stand up by rising straight up. You will see this assumption tested by almost every team that tries the horizontal web. It is great to watch.

I have found that the holes can be a little larger on the horizontal web and still be a challenge. Even if the holes are large the team still has to figure out how to get people from the hole to the far side of the web without disturbing it.

The House

The House

PROPS:
One 30-40 foot rope. A retired climbing rope works well.

OBJECTIVE:
Use a rope to form a house. Emphasizes problem solving and communication techniques.

HISTORY:
Both this activity and the Star come from games I used to play in elementary school. Then, the object was to draw them with a pencil without lifting the lead or retracing a line.

INSTRUCTIONS:
Ask the group to pick up the rope. Tell them they can slide their hands along the rope, but they can't let go and/or trade places in the line. Their task is to 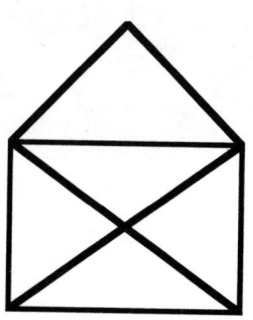 form a house or an envelope, whichever they prefer, without the rope doubling back on itself. You may need to provide a sketch of the end product for them to see.

The Infinite Circle

The Infinite Circle

PROPS:
4x4 boards or landscape ties cut to various lengths between 4 and 18 inches. The ends of the boards do not have to be cut square, but they shouldn't be pointed or at too great an angle. There needs to be at least one board for each person.

OBJECTIVE:
The team celebrates steps from gathering boards to standing on them to balancing on them while the boards are upright.

HISTORY:
I first experienced this activity at Camp Lutherhoma, near Tahlequah, Oklahoma. I played it with a group without knowing what would happen next. There were enough logs for forty people. I chose a short board, assuming I might have to carry the thing around while I did this "new" activity. Little did I know I would be standing on my board and sharing it with the person to my right.

INSTRUCTIONS:
This activity is about celebrating success. After each accomplishment we will celebrate with a loud "hoooowaaa"! Let's try it, "Hoooowaaa!"

Go to the pile of logs over there and pick out one for yourself, then return here to the circle. (When everyone has accomplished this part of the task, celebrate!) "Hoooowaaa!"

Everyone step towards the center of the circle one step and set the logs on the ground at your feet. (When that's done) "Hoooowaaa!"

Everyone stand on your logs with no one touching the ground. If you start to lose your balance, step off rather than fall off. You can always try it again. (When that's done) "Hoooowaaa!"

81

While you're up and with no one touching the ground, move one log to your left. (When that's done) "Hoooowaaa!"

While you're up and with no one touching the ground, move two more logs to the left. (When that's done) "Hoooowaaa!"

While everyone is up off the ground, get one person to balance on his up-ended log without anyone stepping onto the ground. (When that's done) "Hoooowaaa!"

Let's go for two up-ended logs. (When that's done) "Hoooowaaa!"

How many can we do? Three more? All? (After each person uprights a log) "Hoooowaaa!"

FACILITATOR NOTES:
The energy and attitude of the facilitator can make this activity an exhilarating challenge or a chore. Make it fun and lively.

The instructions I have here take the group from selecting their logs to balancing everyone on all the uprighted logs. Use good judgment when working with your participants. Getting everyone to balance on the logs lying on the ground may be a major accomplishment. The point is to take the group one step beyond where they thought they could go.

Safety is always on my mind when people are balancing on anything. Encourage breaks in between attempts and let people know that it's okay to step off and try again rather than "going for it all" and falling.

Fifteen people in a group would be a maximum for this activity. People invariably lean on one another to keep balanced. If there are too many people in a group you lose that closeness. If you have more people, just divide into more groups.

Lines Of Communication

Lines Of Communication

PROPS:

The device consists of a flattened Frisbee (keep the lip side down), six eye screws, six 20-foot parachute cords and six metal rings tied to trees, table legs, or a specially designed PVC structure as seen below. Each parachute cord runs from a participant's hand, through a ring, through an eye screw, through an adjacent ring, and back to a participant. The adjacent cords share a ring at each ring site.

OBJECTIVE:

The basic goal of the activity is to use a special device provided to drop a ball into a container.

PREPARATION:

If you do not have the PVC structure shown below, find a location to tie a circle of rope approximately 3.5 feet high and no more than 8 feet in diameter with nothing inside the circle. Table legs or a small grove of trees work well. Attach the rings to the rope at equal distances around the circle. Place the flattened Frisbee with eye screws in the middle of the circle. Thread each of the six cords from the outside of the circle through a ring, through an eye screw, through an adjacent ring, and back to the outside of the circle. Tie a quick slip knot to join the two loose ends of the cord. The slip knot will keep the cords from unthreading as you thread the other five cords. Everything should look symmetrical and untangled. Now place a one gallon bucket or some other container inside the circle approximately 2 feet from the center, then put the ball on the Frisbee.

With the PVC structure the set-up process is the same except that the rings are easier to attach and the structure is exactly what you need where you need it. The structure can be ordered using the form at the back of the book.

INSTRUCTIONS:

Participants may not touch the cords inside the parameter of rings or the rings themselves. Of course no one can touch the ball or the Frisbee it's on. If the ball rolls off the Frisbee and contacts the ground, terrible things occur to the people closest to the ball (e.g., blindness, muteness, trading cords with someone else but standing in the same place, etc.)

SCENARIO:

You have been selected as the best team to save the world. Every two thousand years a "seed of all knowledge" germinates and supplies the world with new information and insight for the next two millennia. Unfortunately the seed has rolled from its protective pod and may potentially inject knowledge and insight too soon and too quickly. As a result, libraries around the world may ignite and skulls may rupture from the information overload. Only this team remains as a last hope for the planet.

A group of research scientists and naturalists began the first steps in the rescue process, but were distracted by the Nobel Prize ceremonies and an endangered species in Montana. They left their specially developed device with the seed of knowledge resting on its anti-germination pad. It is true that "knowledge is power" so the seed is extremely powerful. If the seed was to leave the anti-germination pad (fall off, roll off) before you deposited it back into its pod, terrible consequences would occur to team members in the seed's nearest vicinity.

Use the strings of the device left by the previous group to deposit the seed into its pod. A note left on the device said that nothing should get closer to the seed than the outside of the device's frame. Touching the seed or the anti-germination pad causes instant death. Good luck!

FACILITATOR NOTES:

Lines of communication is an activity that challenges several people to work together towards a common goal. Unlike many other activities, this one cannot be done easier by fewer people.

At least three participants are required and up to 12 people may take part in the action. When all six cords are threaded the game will accommodate six people, each with both ends of the same cord, or up to twelve people, each with one end of a cord. If you had only four people you could thread only four cords and eliminate the other two.

Coordinating efforts is often an issue discovered by the team. If even one person acts independently, the ball will drop regardless of the intentions of the rest of the team (a challenge for interdependence).

When the ball drops off the Frisbee, the facilitator can return the ball to its place.

It has been my experience in at least three instances that a team took approximately 30 seconds to deliver the ball into the bucket. Was it luck??? I didn't panic however, I pulled a different ball from my bag of tricks and announced that they had handled the test "seed" extremely well and now it was time for the real thing. It took them the "usual" thirty minutes to complete the activity.

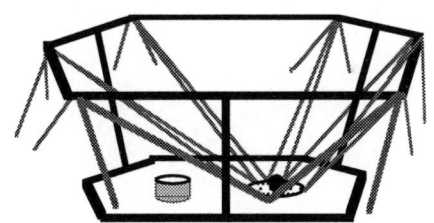

Variation:
Eliminate the ball from the activity. Take paper plates, give them dollar values (both negative and positive values) and place them in the playing area inside the circle or hexagon. Put a loop of masking tape on each plate so that the Frisbee can pick them off the floor if it is set on a plate. Inform the team they have 15 minutes, once they start, to make as much money as they can. Negative and positive amounts are totaled to show the remaining profit. To make money plates must be picked up by the Frisbee, brought to the edge of the PVC structure and removed by a player.

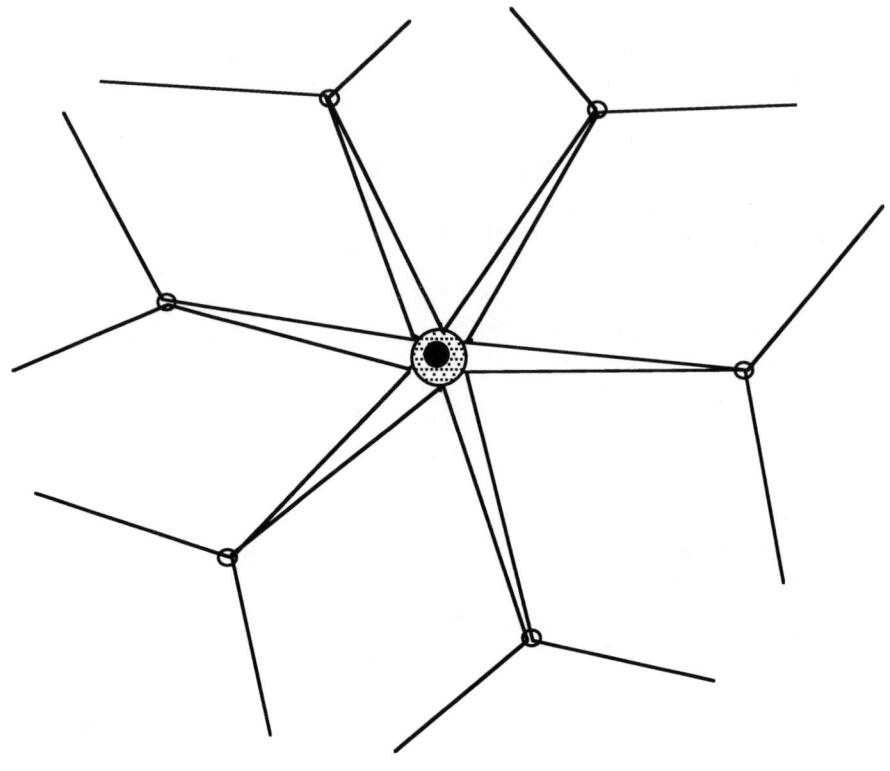

On Target

On Target

INTRODUCTION:
The following series of activities called "On Target" are team initiatives used with a high ropes course. Proper training in the use of a high ropes course is required before facilitating any of the On Target activities.

The three variations of On Target that follow are different enough to be explained separately. The first version is best for a team of up to 12 members. It uses a zip line. The second version also uses a zip line, but is designed more complexly for up to 20 to 30 people. The last version uses a stationary high course event (in this case a pamper pole) and is designed for approximately 12 people.

On Target #1
(For Smaller Team on Zip Line)

PROPS:
Target markers: hula hoops, bright spots, or deck tennis rings.
Balloons, water

OBJECTIVE:
Team uses resources, planning, decision making, and execution to earn money by dropping water balloons from a zip line.

HISTORY:
A phone conversation from a fellow trainer led to the creation of On Target. Joel Cryer, a trainer and ropes course builder out of Austin, Texas told us about a high course team activity he called "Bombs Away". We added a few details and changes that fit with our customer's situation and went for it. The activity proved to be an excellent way of overcoming the individualism of the high course. There were roles for everyone. Those who wanted to stay on the ground could and those who wanted to climb could.

PREPARATION:

Before approaching this activity, expose the team to a high ropes course event. Teach them how to team belay (see team belay instructions in this book) including all ground hook-ups and safety procedures for participants who climb on the course. You will be holding the team responsible for the safety procedures during On Target.

Give the On Target instructions and map to the team in advance of the activity.

When you get to the zip line, set out the hula hoops and spots according to the map while another facilitator sets up the zip line equipment. The team can be putting on their harnesses.

Quickly review the safety procedures with the team and teach any others that are specific to the zip line.

Give the team their four balloons and container of water. Start the timer. Any questions related to the solutions to this activity should be purchased by the team at a consultant rate once the timer has begun. If someone (especially the safety team) does not follow the safety procedures you have taught, say "Stop" and do not allow the team to proceed until they fix the problem.

ON TARGET!:
WORKING THE MODEL FOR SUCCESS

You have spent the last several hours defining your model for success. Your opportunity now is to turn that model into action.

Constraints:
You may plan as long as you like this evening. You may use the equipment provided in your evening research and development. You must assign a scribe to note the research and development process to report to your facilitators (Safety Regulation Officers) in the morning.

You will have 10 minutes in the morning at the ON TARGET site to complete your plan. You will have 1 hour to complete the action process.

No team member may walk in the target area until the 1 hour process has begun.

The team may purchase strategic restructuring time for $10,000,000 per minute.

The Safety Regulation Officers (SROs) must approve the plan & are present to monitor all potentially dangerous processes-a "STOP ACTION" from an SRO must immediately stop all action. The SRO can approve or disapprove each step & will provide no other input.

The SROs can become consultants from a consultant firm for an investment of $1,000,000 per minute. The consultant firm can provide more specific information, yet will not be physically involved in the solution.

The Challenge:

Use up to 4 of your team members to drop 4 water balloons unassisted into the team's choice of the targets below the high zip line. Each target has a value of from $50,000,000 to $999,000,000.

The zip line safety equipment will be installed by the SRO team during the 10 minute on site planning time. One SRO will be on the zip platform and at least one SRO will be on the ground.

On Target Map

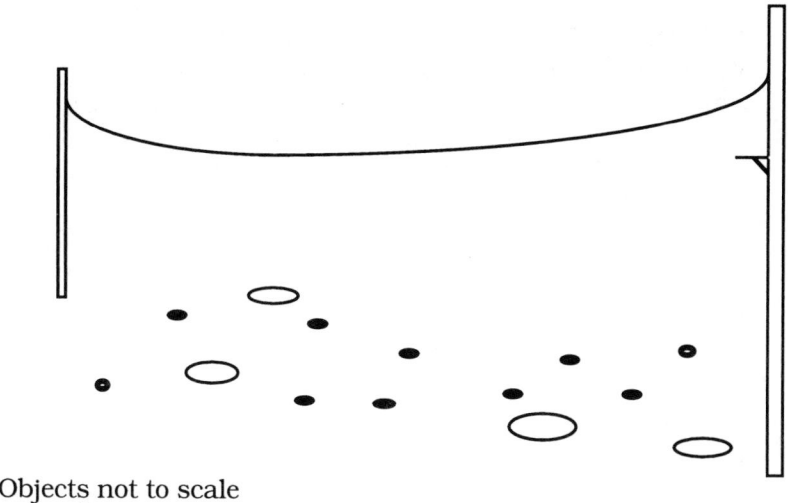

Objects not to scale

$ in millions

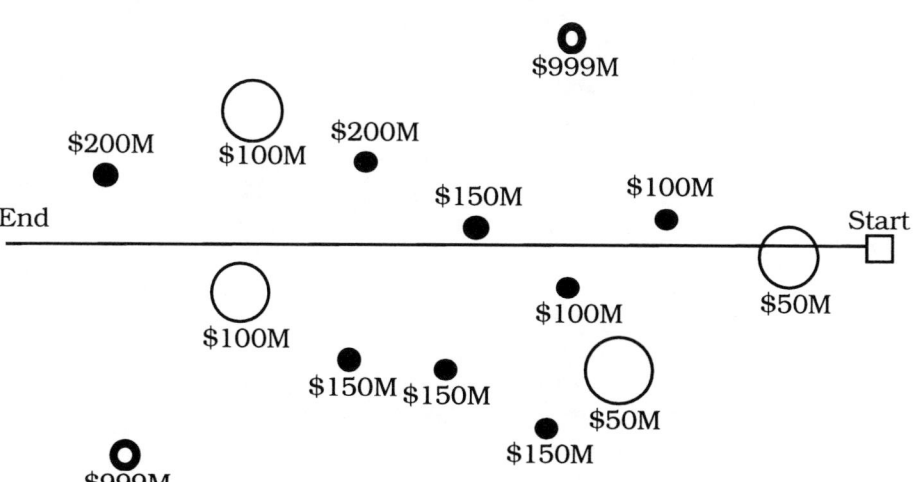

On Target #2
(For Larger Team on Zip Line)

PROPS:
Target markers: hula hoops, bright 8 1/2" spots or deck tennis rings

Projectiles: 10 balloons, 5 eggs, 5 sheets of paper, 5 tennis balls

Projectile materials: At least two gallons of water, 5 packages of straws, 3 rolls of masking tape.

OBJECTIVE:
Team uses its resources, planning, decision making, and execution to earn money by dropping projectiles from the zip line.

HISTORY:
The scenario is geared for an healthcare organization that happens to be the inspiration for this activity. The first group we used this activity with had 24 players. The time seemed to be more than enough in the beginning, then approximately half-way through the initiative, there was a rush to send climbers down the zip line to deliver the shots. Creative problem solving paid off with each toss. In the remaining 10 seconds before the timer sounded, the CFO of the company tossed what projectiles he had from the platform at the targets scoring $10,400! The event fulfilled its purpose of bringing members of management and staff together to practice their skills around problem solving and interpersonal interactions organizationally.

PREPARATION:
Before approaching this activity, expose the team to a high ropes course event. Teach them how to team belay (see team belay instructions in this book) including all ground hook-ups and safety procedures for participants who climb on the course. You will be holding the team responsible for the safety procedures during On Target.

Give the On Target instructions and map to the team in when you get to the zip line site. Tell them they can have planning time while the facilitators do the equipment set ups, however, no materials may be touched and no one can walk into the On Target area.

When you get to the zip line, set out the hula hoops and spots according to the map while another facilitator sets up the zip line equipment. A facilitator on the ground should start reviewing the safety procedures with the safety/transportation team as soon as they are chosen.

When the Safety Regulation Officers (facilitators) are prepared, give the team their materials and start the timer. Any questions related to the solutions to this activity should be purchased by the team at a consultant rate once the timer has begun. If someone (especially the safety team) does not follow the safety procedures you have taught, say "Stop" and do not allow the team to proceed until they fix the problem.

ON TARGET!:
WORKING THE MODEL FOR SUCCESS

You have spent several months defining your model for success. Your opportunity now is to turn that model into action. What is required in this initiative is neither easy nor clear-cut. . . but neither is the real world.

Several large contracts and the income they provide are potentially yours. To land a contract for a particular population, you must demonstrate that your facilities are "On Target" by delivering a client to a designated treatment site. To realize a payment for your services and prove that your services are effective, each client must end up showing results (i.e., not breaking or blowing away, etc.)

Use the attached map to determine net income based on where the client is placed. Every referral that has been accurately placed (hits a target), earns the company $200 and lands you a contract for services that may result in much more income.

Constraints:

You may use your time as you best see fit. You may only use the equipment provided.

The safety regulation officers (SROs) must approve the safety of plan & are present to monitor all potentially dangerous processes -- a "STOP ACTION" from an SRO must immediately stop all action. The SRO can approve or disapprove each step & will provide no other input.

No team member may walk in the target area until the 75 minute process has begun. The timer starts whenever the SROs are ready.

The SROs can become consultants for an investment of $1,000 per minute. The consultants can provide more specific information, yet will not be physically involved in the solution.

The Challenge:

Use some your team members to drop water balloons, eggs, regular balloons, tennis balls, and airplanes into the team's choice of the targets below the high zip line. Each target has a value of from $5,000 to $90,000. For drops to count, they must be unassisted and dropped/thrown by the Zipper.

The zip line safety equipment has been installed by the SRO team. One SRO will be on the platform and at least one other will be on the ground.

Official roles:

- •• Management   (at least 2 people)
- •• Accounting   (at least one person)
- •• Safety/Transportation up   (at least 4 people)
- •• Staff   (divide people into specialist teams)

Clients	Placement	Effectiveness ($)	Tools
* eggs	hit target,	keep from breaking,	straws and tape
* tennis balls	hit target,	stops in a target (5 sec)	straws and tape
* water balloons	hit target,	must break	straws and tape
* aired-up balloon	hit target,	stops in a target (5 sec)	straws and tape
* paper airplane	hit target,	stops in a target (5 sec)	straws and tape

Roles may be changed with management approval.

Management (at least 2 people)

Do what managers effectively do.

Accounting (at least one person)

Keep track of money earned.

Safety/Transportation (at least 4 people)

In charge of safely getting people up to the crow's nest so they can go for a target. Team belay is required as well as helmets, harnesses, commands, etc.

The Egg Unit

Your specialty is working with eggs

Your team gets $200 each time you hit a target from the zip line.
The dollar amount indicated on the map is earned if the egg does not break when it lands.
Your only resources are straws, tape, and yourselves.

The Tennis Ball Unit

Your specialty is working with tennis balls

Your team gets $200 each time you hit a target from the zip line.
The dollar amount indicated on the map is earned if the ball stays in/on a target for at least 5 seconds.
Your only resources are straws, tape, and yourselves.

The Water Balloon Unit

Your specialty is working with water balloons

Your team gets $200 each time you hit a target from the zip line.
The dollar amount indicated on the map is earned if the balloon breaks upon impact.
Your only resources are straws, tape, and yourselves.

The Aired-up Balloon Unit

Your specialty is working with air balloons filled at least 6 inches in diameter.
Your team gets $200 each time you hit a target from the zip line.
The dollar amount indicated on the map is earned if the balloon stays in/on a target for at least 5 seconds.
Your only resources are straws, tape, and yourselves.

The Paper Airplane Unit

Your specialty is working with paper airplanes

Your team gets $200 each time you hit a target from the zip line.
The dollar amount indicated on the map is earned if the plane stays in/on a target for at least 5 seconds.
Your only resources are straws, tape, and yourselves.

On Target Map

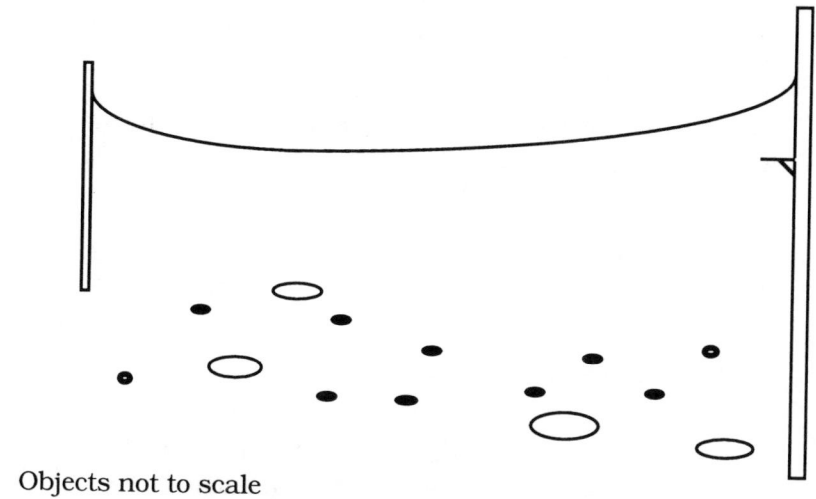

Objects not to scale

$ in thousands

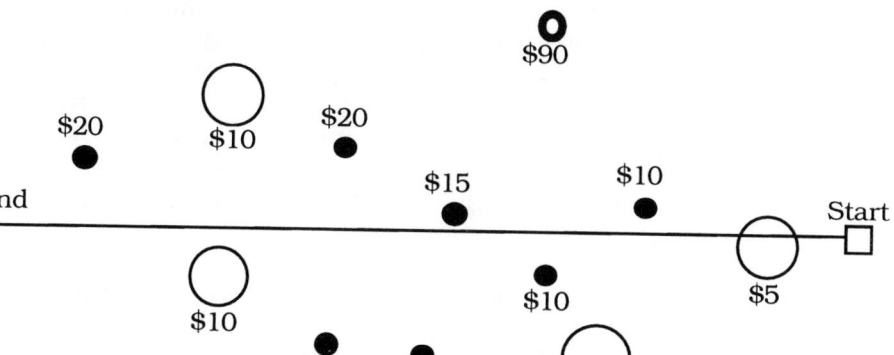

On Target #3
(For Smaller Team on High Course)

PROPS:
Target markers: hula hoops, bright spots or deck tennis rings
Projectiles: 6 balloons, 4 eggs
Projectile materials: water, straws, bubble gum, roll of masking tape, box of paper clips, cups, scissors, paper, etc.

OBJECTIVE:
Team uses resources, planning, decision making, and execution to earn money by dropping water balloons and eggs from a high course element.

HISTORY:
We wrote this particular version for a team of scientists. The team was moving into using self-directed work teams and determining how they should be coached/managed. The safety team played the role of a coach team while the small groups played the role of self-directed work teams. We did not have access to a zip line for this activity, so I changed the target layout and some of the dynamics of the usual On Target strategies. By the way, from 27 feet in the air a hoop is harder to hit than it looks and an egg protection device tends to blow in the breeze.

PREPARATION:
Give the On Target instructions and map to the team. Read it aloud to the whole group.

Divide the team into its sub teams and start the 30 minute timer. Take the safety team outside to teach them how to do a team belay and conduct safety procedures while the other sub teams work on their eggs, balloons, and strategies.

Teach the safety team how to team belay (see team belay instructions in this book) including all ground hook-ups and safety procedures for participants who climb on the course. You will be holding the safety team responsible for the safety procedures during On Target.

Go to the On Target site when the 30 minutes have expired. The sub teams should have all of their containers prepared already.

Tell them they can have additional planning time while the facilitators do the equipment set ups, however, no one can walk into the On Target area. Set out the hula hoops and spots according to the map while another facilitator sets up the high course equipment.

When the Safety Regulation Officers (facilitators) are prepared, start the one hour timer. Any questions related to the solutions to this activity should be purchased by the team at a consultant rate once the timer has begun. If someone (especially the safety team) does not follow the safety procedures you have taught, say "Stop" and do not allow the team to proceed until they fix the problem.

ON TARGET!:
WORKING THE MODEL FOR SUCCESS

You are defining your model for success. Your opportunity now is to assemble that model and put it into action. What is required in this initiative is neither easy nor clear-cut. . . but neither is the real world.

Research and Development has been asked to test two top secret liquids in a unique way. They must be elevated more than 20 feet above ground and dropped into specially prepared receptacles.

Each receptacle has special properties and some will potentially create more of a profit for the organization than others. Unfortunately, the higher income producers are harder to test.

You will have 30 minutes initially for drop teams to prepare for the tests and a safety team to receive specialized safety training. Drop teams can only use the special materials provided.

Everyone will have one hour for testing after the preparation time has ended.

Using effective interpersonal and practical techniques, maximize profits.

Constraints:
You may use your time within each stage of the process as you best see fit. You may only use the equipment provided.

The Safety Regulation Officers (SROs) must approve the safety of the plan & are present to monitor all potentially dangerous processes -- a "STOP ACTION" from an SRO must immediately stop all action. The SROs can approve or disapprove each step and will provide no other input.

No team member may walk in the target area until the 60 minute process has begun. The timer starts whenever the SROs are ready.

The SROs can become consultants for an investment of $2,000 per minute. The consultants can provide more specific information, yet will not be physically involved in the solution.

The Challenge:
Use some your team members to drop "water balloons" or "eggs" into the targets below the high course. Each target has a value of from $2,000 to $99,000. For drops to count, they must be unassisted and dropped/thrown by the Climber.

The safety equipment has been installed by the SRO team. The SROs will be on the ground.

Safety/Coach Team
In charge of safely getting people up to the crow's nest so they can go for a target. Team belay is required as well as helmets, harnesses, commands, etc.

Act as a management team for the other testing teams. Define your own roles within the organization and within your team.

The Egg & Water Balloon Teams
Your specialty is working with "eggs" and "water balloons".

The "Egg" Samples
The dollar amount indicated on the map is earned if the egg does not break when it lands.

The "Water Balloon" Samples

The dollar amount indicated on the map is earned if the balloon breaks upon impact.

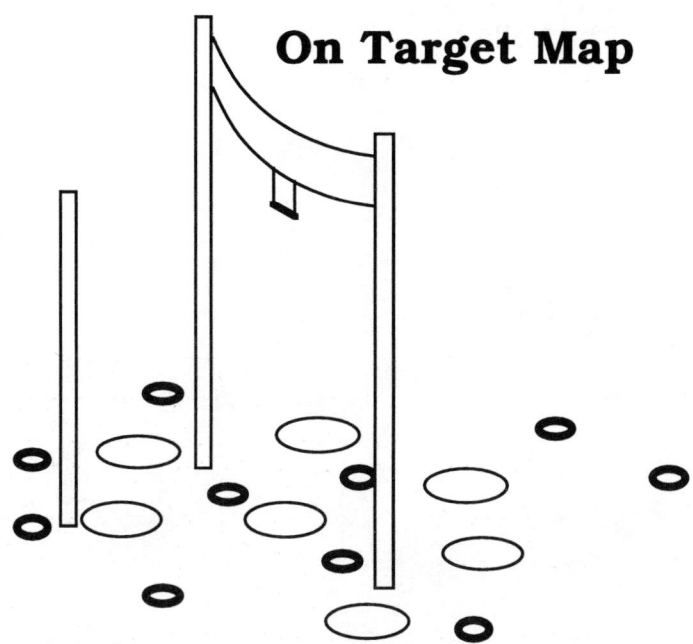

On Target Map

Objects not to scale.

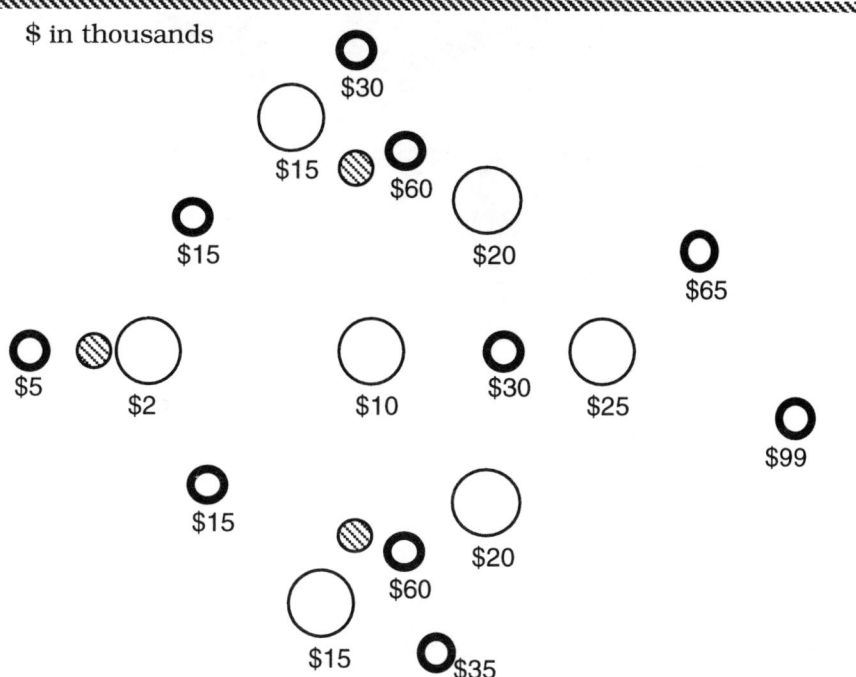

$ in thousands

$30
$15
$60
$15
$20
$65
$5
$2
$10
$30
$25
$99
$15
$20
$60
$15
$35

Oogly

Oogly: A Metaphor For Change

PROPS:
Three to four pounds of corn starch, a large unbreakable bowl, water

OBJECTIVE:
Corn starch mixed with water has strange properties. It behaves as a solid when it has pressure applied to it and it behaves as a liquid without pressure applied to it. Besides being neat to play with, oogly provides a memorable illustration of what happens when an organization is forced into a change process.

HISTORY:
I first heard of this mixture in 1994 at a conference in Cincinnati, Ohio. My partner and I were providing activities for the Association for Quality and Participation when a woman told us about how she used the stuff in some of her training workshops. It sounded great so when I got home I bought a pound and tried it out. Since then I have whitened many floors with the stuff. Fortunately, when the oogly dries, it sweeps or vacuums right up. Hands are easy to clean as well.

PREPARATION:
Pour your dry corn starch into a bowl then add water. It takes almost as much water as corn starch, but mix-in the water by hand about a 1/2 cup at a time to avoid adding too much water. You can tell when enough water has been added because all the powder forms into a stiff liquid. Mixing this stuff can be hard work. Avoid trying to stir it too quickly because it resists change and will wear you out (now there's a metaphor). If you add too much water, just let the mixture set for a few minutes and pour off the excess water that settles at the top.

If you plan to use this stuff more than one day, you might add a tablespoon or two of bleach. Bacteria from people's hands will start to grow a culture if you aren't careful.

METAPHORS:

Oogly resists change. You can punch it or poke it forcefully and it will resist your force completely. Only when you work at its speed does it accept your hands. Sometimes it even feels as if it is welcoming you in with a gentle tug.

Once you have penetrated the surface you can draw out a piece and mold it. As long as you keep it moving by providing constant energy, it will stay together. Provide too much energy and it fractures and breaks apart; provide too little energy and it drools back into its container and looks just like it did before you took it out.

Pass a ball of oogly from person to person. If anyone hesitates, it puddles. People discover a balance of energy that will keep the oogly intact and not wear them out.

As the mixture dries, it becomes more easily fractured and ultimately turns to powder. If too much water is added, it becomes unmanageable and sloppy. Water isn't bad, but too much or too little can cause problems.

Some people enjoy adding several drops of food coloring to the mixture after it has been thoroughly mixed because it looks "cool" and it illustrates how difficult it is to totally integrate something new into a system that resists change.

Other Suggestions:
Take a ball of oogly and throw it onto a table or on the floor. It bounces then puddles.

Forcefully rub the surface of the oogly. It fractures to the bottom of the container.

Try quickly tossing the container of oogly on someone. It stays inside the bowl (at least that has been my experience).

Stick a straw into the mixture and try to pull it out quickly. It resists.

I have not tried it yet, but I want to fill a wading pool with oogly and play around with running across the surface!

Photo Finish

Photo Finish

PROPS:
Rope for start or finish line (optional), Polaroid camera (optional)

OBJECTIVE:
Everyone on a team crosses a finish line at exactly the same time.

PREPARATION:
Find a location that has approximately 30 feet between a starting line and a finish line. A sidewalk or a straight rope line works well. Give the instructions to the team and stand at the finish line.

INSTRUCTIONS:
This activity is called photo finish. Everyone must start behind the starting line and go toward the finish line and cross the finish line at exactly the same time. If someone finishes before or after anyone else, the whole team tries again from behind the starting line. The team has an unlimited number of tries.

OBSERVATIONS:
Most teams create a sense of urgency from the starting line to the finish. The truth is that time is not an important factor in this initiative.

Teams generally take about six "runs" before they finish simultaneously. If you want to pull yourself out of the judge role, ask for a volunteer from the team to watch at the finish line and determine the all-way tie.

A Polaroid camera or video camera is great to use and show the team later. One of the amazing things that I have noticed each time I have facilitated this activity is how far off the perceptions of the team can be. In some cases a person will finish two or three feet before the rest of the team and the whole team will believe they finished together.

This activity seems too simple at first thought. Many organizations face similar situations all the time and realize too late that coordinating people can be a difficult achievement. For example, businesses try to provide training for everyone within a short time span, or a complex project needs to have everyone finish their deadlines in a coordinated fashion. In those situations the same factors that create success in the photo finish will create success in real situations.

Plastic Wrap

Plastic Wrap

TIME:
10 minutes

PROPS:
A roll of very inexpensive plastic wrap cut to four inches wide.

OBJECTIVE:
A group moves from one side of a room to another as fast as they can as a unit wrapped by plastic wrap. Icebreaker, gets people close, sets tone for creative problem solving, fun!

HISTORY:
A friend and fellow instructor, Barbara Bowles, created this activity for a youth group she was facilitating in Tulsa. I borrowed the idea and have used it for my corporate customers as a fun, quick metaphor for stretching goals and limits.

INSTRUCTIONS:
Ask everyone in the group to gather in a tight clump, shoulder to shoulder. Take the four inch wide roll of plastic wrap and begin wrapping it around the whole group at about waist height. Make about 5 rounds while emphasizing to the group that they should not break the band holding them together and they should not take it off the group.

Once they are wrapped up, ask them how fast they think they can get from one side of the room and touch the other side of the room. When they have guessed, time their travel and celebrate the effort regardless. Ask them if they could travel the same distance in a shorter time. "Yes" is almost always immediately the reply. Time them again when they have problem solved enough.

Usually the time has shortened significantly, but they are resistant to make another run.

Ask everyone to move to the center of the room and back away from the center of the circle until the band breaks or they just can't move back anymore. When you use good stretchy plastic wrap, the circle often stretches 30 feet in diameter or more and people see that they just had to stretch their boundaries to accomplish their goal.

Variation:
Place three objects in three separate locations. Put them far enough apart so that the whole group has to move from place to place to touch each one as quickly as possible. Emphasis that they should not break the band. When their time is as low as they want, ask them to stretch the band. Hopefully you placed the objects in such a way that all three can be touched simultaneously.

Portable Zig-Zag

Portable Zig-Zag

PROPS:
Three portable zig-zag boards, at least fourteen 8 1/2 inch rubber or carpet spots

Each of the three zig zag boards consists of a long 2X4 board, two eight-inch 2X4 boards, two eight inch in diameter circular boards, and a four-inch 2X4 and with a four-inch piece of board from the same type of wood as the circles. All the pieces are fastened together with dry wall screws. (See illustration below) Each long 2X4 board is a different length. I use five-foot, 5 1/2-foot, and six-foot boards.

OBJECTIVE:
Team uses the zig-zag boards to travel from point A to point B on the spots without touching the ground.

HISTORY:
The zig-zag is a favorite team initiative. (see Silver Bullets by Karl Rohnke, page 124) Mary Todd and I thought of several wild ideas of how to make this low course element a portable initiative. Each idea seemed to be more material intensive and more complex. The stumps that are buried in the ground gave us the most trouble. We kept thinking of ways to build portable stumps in a way so that they would not fall over. The light bulbs went off when we thought of movable stumps and markers placed where they had to go. I made the first prototype in my garage and used them with a team. Many teams later, I still have the original zig-zag boards.

PREPARATION:
Place spots on the floor at intervals that will exactly match your beams. A bit of masking tape under each spot will help it stay in place. The spots will be placed in pairs, side-by-side, except for the single spot at the beginning and the end.

A pattern of long-short-medium-long-medium-short-medium (14 spots) works well in most spaces and gives the activity a variety of dynamics such as planning, space issues, individualism vs. teamwork, etc. Feel free to place the spots around corners to increase the communication difficulty and make the end of the journey a surprise.

INSTRUCTIONS:
The team members cannot touch the ground and the beams cannot touch the ground. The spots protect the beam pads from the ground, but the stationery spots cannot be touched by the participants. Spots cannot be moved.
The whole team must cross from here to there maintaining physical contact the whole way. "Deaths" and terrible effects may be eliminated by everyone starting over.

SCENARIO:
Lucky for you, the disaster plan was in place. The beaker that just broke on your laboratory floor contained a rare virus that has strange effects on humans. One characteristic of the virus is that it grows rapidly and any contact can cause infection.

Using the safety equipment provided for just such an emergency, make your way to safety. Be certain that you use the equipment properly. Any contact with the floor could contaminate the equipment and expose team members to the virus from the tainted gear.

The chemical stepping stones that have emerged from the floor of the lab are highly toxic to the virus (and to anything else). Fortunately, your safety equipment does not react to the steps. Just don't touch or try to move the chemical stepping stones.

The virus is spreading quickly. In approximately 10 minutes it will start spreading toward the uncontaminated flooring on which you are now standing. Get started.

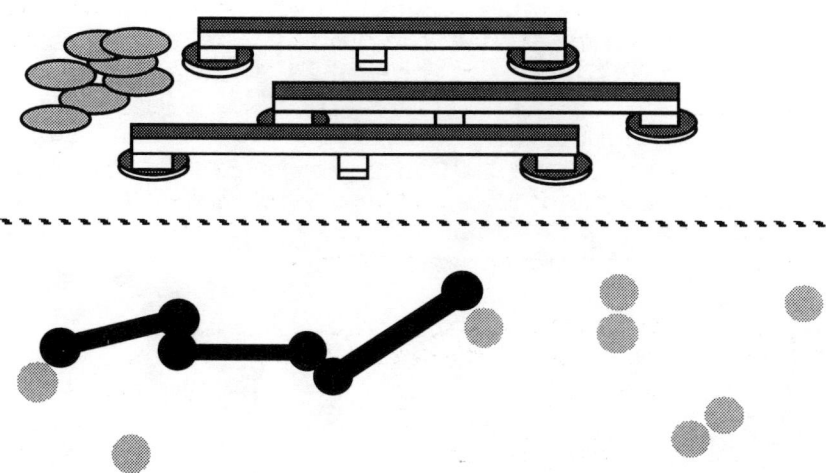

Puff-O-War

Puff-O-War

PROPS:
Bowl of extra firm gelatin (your choice of flavors), 8 feet of 5/8 inch clear tubing for each pair of competitors.

OBJECTIVE:
Blow gelatin through a clear plastic tube into your competitor's mouth.

HISTORY:
Who knows where this truly gross game came from? I started thinking of this game several years ago, while I had too much free time. The original thought was to use a raw egg instead of gelatin. I bought some tubing and mixed-up some unflavored gelatin (I had some lying around.) and added some sweetener and blue dye. Then I located some unsuspecting friends to try it. We had lots of fun with it in spite of losing some gelatin in their couch.

Later that month I presented the puff-o-war to a group at the 1993 annual OTRA conference. Believe it or not we had several "takers". It was a memorable experience for everyone. People still talk about the relief of the victories and the agony of the defeats.

PREPARATION:
If you ever do an activity like this, make sure to have everything done in advance. Clean the tubes with bleach water and allow them to dry and look clean. Use a permanent marker or some tape to mark the middle of the tubing.

Mix the gelatin with at least half the water listed on the instructions. It is like making Knox Blox®. The gelatin should be approximately one inch thick so that when you "cookie cutter" it with the tubing, it will form a plug of gelatin one inch long. Cutting the plug with the tube can be tricky. I have had the best results when I push the tube slowly to the bottom of the gelatin container and then move the cutting edge of the tube to the side so it will unstick the gelatin from the bottom of the container.

GAME INSTRUCTIONS:

* Find two willing contestants.

* One of the contestants should either suck or blow the plug to the middle of the tube.

* Standing face to face, each contestant should hold on to an end of the tube and get ready.

* A third person counts, "One, two, three, Go!"

* On "go" both try to blow the plug of gelatin into the other's mouth.

* Whoever blows the plug beyond the far end of the tube is the winner.

* Clean the tube between duels.

Variation:

Try it cowboy style, so that both contestants start with a hand at their sides and "draw". This variation makes for some fast contests because the plug can move so rapidly.

Quality Journey

Quality Journey

PROPS:
You will need several things for this activity. A copy of the Quality Journey Template, seven blank envelopes, a roll of masking tape, a harness or rope for each person, a six or seven foot length of rope, a carabiner for each person, a ball approximately three feet in diameter, bandannas, a map of the journey area (can be hand drawn), a pair of scissors

OBJECTIVE:
Transport a ball by following instructions placed at predetermined locations. This activity teaches concepts common to Total Quality Management in a highly experiential way.

HISTORY:
Several years ago Mary Todd and I worked for a company that was adopting Quality as a way of doing business. We worked with the upper managers who were designing a roll-out plan for implementing Quality. The roll-out plan gave us the idea of keeping the quality ball rolling. The activity was not easy, but people got the concepts of what it was that would make the implementation a success. We have tried this activity with several other companies since. It has always made a significant impact with the teams.

PREPARATION:
Gather your materials in advance. This activity is designed to be experienced outside, however, it could be done indoors with the right facilities. Allow yourself an hour for preparation.

Map the locations for the journey. Each location will have an instruction slip and an envelop with further instructions inside it. I try to keep Points A - E in a circular pattern with approximately 200 feet between each point. The natural layout of the campus may determine the actual placement of the envelopes.

Take the Quality Journey template and fill-in the blanks with the various locations you determined, then cut the papers into strips where indicated. Be careful not to mix-up the strips. An envelope or statement out of sequence could be disastrous (A fear I have had often). Take the quote I have provided, or get one of your own, and cut it into five puzzle pieces. Stuff each envelope with a puzzle piece and an "inside" further instructions slip. Don't put a quote piece inside the Point D 1/2 envelope since the team could skip that one. Attach instructions to the appropriate envelopes with some tape and then place each instruction/envelope at its location. The first instructions should be handed to the team after you have connected them.

Inflate the ball. I have used a 3' beach ball many times. Stick a strip of tape to the ball that says "Quality". The ball will represent quality to the team.

Gather the participants and harness them. Tie a rope into a circle about half the size of a hula hoop. Connect the participants to the circle of rope with carabiners by hooking it in the rear of their harness. You should end up with a tight cluster of people hooked together facing outward from the middle.

Hand the group the first set of instructions with its envelope, the map, and the ball. Stay close by to clarify instructions and spot for potential safety concerns. Once the team has its mission statement, the activity should speak for itself. In other words, don't tell the team any more than you have to and let them monitor their own performance. Everything that happens on their journey will be great for the debrief later.

As the team heads toward point D, a new member needs to be added to the group. The member can be anyone not already connected.

OBSERVATIONS:
Some great things about this activity are the metaphors. The team starts off connected but facing outward. As they travel on the journey they learn

about how to work together and accommodate special needs. At the same time the team learns how to implement quality -- by guiding quality and keeping it under control, sharing the load, being honest, caring for each other, orienting new people, etc.

QUALITY JOURNEY MISSION STATEMENT

Importance to this team:

Officials monitoring candidates for the Malcolm Baldridge National Quality Award are evaluating your team in order to publish their findings the task before you is of the utmost in the American Quality Journal, an internationally read journal. The press could make or break your organization depending on your performance.

YOUR TASK:
• Use the attached map (vision) to find the various locations where you will gather pieces of a quote and follow further instructions (missions).
• While traveling, you must take quality (the ball) with you.
• Remain connected as a group (this is a team).
• You have only 1 hour to complete your entire journey.
• Open the first envelope to begin your journey.

✂••••••••••••••••••••••••••✂••••••••••••••••••••••••✂•••••••••••

inside starting envelope

REMAINING ATTACHED TO EACH OTHER, FIND YOUR NEXT INSTRUCTIONS ON THE
_____ (POINT   A).

✂••••••••••••••••••••••••••✂••••••••••••••••••••••••✂•••••••••••

POINT A   -   _____

• IF QUALITY WAS LIFTED IN THE AIR OR
DRAGGED (CONTROLLED RATHER THAN

GUIDED), FOUR PEOPLE MUST
CONTINUOUSLY CROSS THEIR ARMS AND
REPLY "WOULDN'T YOU LIKE TO KNOW" TO
ALL QUESTIONS ASKED OF THEM.

• IF QUALITY WAS KEPT ROLLING AND LEFT
ON THE GROUND (GUIDED, NOT
CONTROLLED), 3 PEOPLE MAY REPOSITION
THEMSELVES AS LONG AS THEY REMAIN
CONNECTED TO THE GROUP BY A
CARABINER THROUGH A HARNESS LOOP.

CONTINUE   TO   _____
(POINT B).

POINT B   -   _____

BEFORE OPENING THE ENVELOPE, ASK
EACH PERSON TO HONESTLY EVALUATE ON
A 1-10 SCALE HOW WELL THE GROUP HAS
TAKEN CARE OF HIS OR HER COMFORT
SINCE THE BEGINNING OF THE JOURNEY.

1   NO CARE TAKEN; I WAS VERY
            UNCOMFORTABLE
5   I NEVER NOTICED HOW WELL I WAS
            BEING TAKEN CARE OF
10 MY EVERY NEED WAS MET OR EXCEEDED

ASK EACH PERSON TO VERBALIZE HIS/HER
RATING THEN OPEN THE ENVELOPE.

✂●●●●●●●●●●●●●●●●●●●●●✂●●●●●●●●●●●●●●●●●●●●✂●●●●●●●●●●
inside envelope

POINT B

• IF ANYONE RATED CARETAKING LESS THAN 7, SOMEONE MUST LOSE USE OF HIS/HER RIGHT LEG.

• IF EVERYONE RATED CARETAKING AT 7 OR MORE, THE "WOULDN'T YOU LIKE TO KNOW" ILLNESS IS CURED.

CONTINUE TO THE _____
(POINT C)

✂●●●●●●●●●●●●●●●●●●●●●●●●●✂●●●●●●●●●●●●●●●●●●●●✂●●●●●●●●●●
inside envelope

POINT C - _____

• IF QUALITY WAS EVER 2-10 FEET FROM THE GROUP, 1 PERSON IS BLIND.
• IF QUALITY WAS EVER 11-20 FEET FROM THE GROUP, 2 PEOPLE ARE BLIND.
• IF QUALITY WAS EVER 21+ FEET FROM THE GROUP, 3 PEOPLE ARE BLIND.
• IF QUALITY WAS ALWAYS WITHIN 2 FEET OF THE GROUP, 1 PERSON MAY REPOSITION HIMSELF/HERSELF BUT MUST REMAIN CONNECTED TO THE GROUP BY A CARABINER THROUGH A HARNESS LOOP.

(IF DESIRED, A LOSS OF A RIGHT LEG MAY BE SUBSTITUTED FOR ANOTHER BLIND PERSON)

CONTINUE TO _____
(POINT D).

POINT D   -   _____

HONESTLY EVALUATE THE INTEGRITY OF
THIS TEAM FROM THE BEGINNING OF THE
JOURNEY UNTIL NOW USING A 1-10 SCALE.

COME TO A GROUP <u>CONSENSUS</u> OF THE
TEAM'S RATING.

1 NO RULES OR LIMITS WERE FOLLOWED.
5 APPROXIMATELY HALF OF THE RULES
    AND LIMITS WERE FOLLOWED.
10 ALL RULES AND LIMITS WERE FOLLOWED
    WITHOUT COMPROMISE

OPEN THE ENVELOPE ONLY AFTER
REACHING A TEAM CONSENSUS.

inside envelope

POINT D
1)
• IF RATING IS 8 OR BETTER, ALL TEAM
    MEMBERS ARE CURED OF HANDICAPS.
• IF 5-7, ALL LIMITS OR HANDICAPS REMAIN.
• IF 1-4, EVERYONE IS BLIND WITH THE
    EXCEPTION OF 1 MUTE

2)
• IF A NEW MEMBER HAS JOINED THE TEAM
    SINCE THE START OF YOUR JOURNEY,
    DID HE/SHE RECEIVE APPROPRIATE
    ORIENTATION AND TRAINING WHEN
    HE/SHE ENTERED THE GROUP ?

NO - GO TO _____ (POINT D 1/2)
BEFORE CONTINUING TO POINT E
YES - CELEBRATION IS CALLED FOR !!!

CONTINUE TO _____
(POINT E) UNLESS THE TEAM DECIDES TO
SEE WHAT IS AT POINT D 1/2 BECAUSE IT
COULD GIVE THEM MORE INFORMATION.

✂•••••••••••••••••••••••••✂•••••••••••••••••••••••••✂•••••••••••

POINT D 1/2 - _____

WAS LEADERSHIP ON THIS JOURNEY TRULY
SHARED? YES NO
-OR-
DID ONE OR TWO TEAM MEMBERS
DOMINATE THE ACTIVE LEADERSHIP ROLE?

OPEN ENVELOPE AFTER THE TEAM HAS
COME TO A DECISION

✂•••••••••••••••••••••••••✂•••••••••••••••••••••••••✂•••••••••••

inside envelope

YES - SHARED LEADERSHIP - EVERYONE
MAY DETACH FROM EACH OTHER'S
HARNESSES, BUT MUST REMAIN
PHYSICALLY CONNECTED WHILE GOING TO
THE _____ (POINT E)

NO - DOMINATING LEADERSHIP - ONE
PERSON MUST BE CARRIED TO THE
_____ (POINT E), ALL CURRENT
HANDICAPS REMAIN

138

WELCOME BACK TO THE START OF YOUR MISSION AND PROCESS !!!

YOUR LIMITS HAVE BEEN CURED BY DIVINE INTERVENTION.

READ ALOUD YOUR QUOTE.

SILENTLY DISCONNECT YOURSELVES, TAKE OFF YOUR HARNESSES, AND USE YOUR JOURNAL PAGES TO WRITE DOWN INSIGHTS YOU HAD DURING THE JOURNEY.

REMAIN SILENT FOR THE NEXT 15 MINUTES AS YOU MAKE NOTES AND TAKE CARE OF BATHROOM NEEDS, ETC.

MEET BACK AT THE TRAINING TABLE WHEN THE TIME IS UP.

A leader is best when people barely know he exists,
Not so good when people obey and acclaim him;
Worse when they despise him.

*Fail to honor people, and
they fail to honor you;
But a good leader, who talks
little,
When his work is done, his
aim fulfilled,
they will say, "We did this
ourselves."*

Lao Tzo

Quick Mathematical Division

If you ever have a large group to divide into several equal teams, maybe this creative division is for you.

First, circle-up and count off all the way around. Ask everyone to remember their number. Tell the odds to stand in one group and the evens in another.

Go to the "odd" team and tell each of them to take his number and add 1 and divide by 2, then divide the odds and evens.

Go to the even group and tell each one of them to take his number and divide by 2, separate the odds and the evens.

Repeat the process until you have the number of teams you need. It's not the most exciting creative division in the world, but it works and people think a little in the process.

Odds: Add 1 then divide by 2
Evens: Divide by 2

Rock Scientists

Rock Scientists

PROPS:
• Four rocks approximately the size of a baseball

• A table

• Bandanna for each person

OBJECTIVE:
Team members communicate the position of rocks to other team members so that the rock positions can be realigned. Verbal and nonverbal communication must me specific and understood.

HISTORY:
Several years ago, Mary Todd and I decided to add an activity creation piece to our ropes course train-the-trainer. One of the trainee groups created this activity. We have used it several times because of how well it teaches the need for clear communication during planning and implementation.

PREPARATION:
After half of the team has left the room, place the rocks on the table so that their configuration can be replicated.

INSTRUCTIONS:
One half of the group will have 10-15 minutes to memorize the placement of the rocks on the table. They can inspect the rocks visually and by touch. The other half of the team will leave the room for 10-15 minutes.

When the 10-15 minutes are over, the study group should put on blindfolds while the facilitator shuffles the rocks. The other group enters the rock area and attempts to place the rocks in their original positions guided only by the blindfolded half of the team. The blindfolded half of the team cannot get closer than five feet to the rocks.

SCENARIO:

A recent discovery by the World Seismological Federation has brought you all here to this precise location to study and repair the key to all gravity on Earth. Apparently a rock formation has created what we call gravity and the formation is now threatened by a future earthquake.

You are a team of rock scientists sent here to study the current rock formation and then reconstruct the formation after the quake. Because of the danger and importance of this mission, the team will be divided into a study team and a reconstruction team. Best calculations show the earthquake occurring within the next 15 minutes. Divide yourselves into two groups. The reconstruction team should leave the area until the earthquake is over. The study team should remain here until the earthquake occurs to memorize the current formation.

(10-15 minutes later)

The earthquake has occurred and has disrupted the rock formation. Without warning, a flash of energy from the rocks has caused the whole study team to lose their eye sight. If you stay at least five feet from the rocks more catastrophic injuries can be avoided.

(The facilitator scrambles the rocks on the table and brings the reconstruction team into the room.)

The study team has memorized the rock formation and was blinded during the earthquake. The reconstruction team's job is now to reposition the rocks into their original formation before the lack of gravity causes world destruction in 15 minutes.

Sardines

Sardines Scenario

PROPS:
Bandannas

OBJECTIVE:
Everyone tries to find the lead sardine while they are blind and only able to say "toy boat".

HISTORY:
I used to play sardines as a kid at church. We would hide in the church building at night with all the lights off. It is amazing how scary a quiet, empty church building can be.

Approximately four years ago Mary Todd and I needed a fun activity for an Amoco group we worked with. I decided to make-up a scenario to make the game more interesting. We didn't play in an enclosed room or with blindfolds. I cut slips of paper with the word "rock" on each of the them except one that had "shark" on it. We secretly drew the slips and went outside. The idea was for the lead sardine (the person with the shark slip) to sneak away while the rest of the sardines walked around the five acres and noticed someone missing. Thirty minutes into it, we realized that the lead sardine might never hide and we would never know. An hour later, two of us discovered we were alone. Panicked we ran around searching for the hiding group. It wasn't too hard; they were talking and laughing.

PREPARATION:
Use an open room so that people have space for wandering blindly. Remove everyone from the room and give them the scenario. Ask everyone to put on their blindfolds. When everyone is sightless, pick a lead sardine to go hide in the room (The lead sardine can see.)

Be sure to spot the people as they walk around and close the doors to the room or you might lose someone.

OBSERVATIONS:

People who are selected as the lead sardine usually start to hide in a small place on the edge of the room. I have noticed that blind sardines generally search the walls of the room first and journey out into the open space less often. I will usually suggest that the lead sardine stand still in the middle of the room.

When the first few people find the lead sardine, I tug on their blindfolds to let them know that it's okay to silently watch and snicker.

The real fun comes when the last people who are still calling out for their fellow schoolmates realize that it's getting really quiet out there. The last sardine usually finds the school by hearing escaped snorts from the tightly grouped sighted sardines.

SARDINES

Of all marine life, the sardine is one of the least understood.

Little known sardine facts:

Sardines are blind.

They are very sensitive to their surroundings. For example they can sense the difference between a rock or seaweed and a shark.

You have probably heard the phrase "Packed-in like sardines." Most people think it came from the way sardines come packed in a can you would buy at the grocery store. Actually, this phrase refers to the way sardines hide when they are in danger. When the lead sardine senses danger (e.g., a shark) it hides in a safe place where the other sardines can also hide. So they squeeze into a single location and are really packed-in.

Sardines communicate with a one-sound vocabulary. When a sardine wants to locate his school, he makes a noise that sounds like "toy boat!" Whenever another sardine hears this sound he must respond "toy boat!" so that all the sardines can know where the others are located. Unfortunately for the less sensitive sardines in the school, a sardine in hiding will not respond to a "toy boat" call because predators might find the hiding school. Less sensitive sardines may be eaten as a result, but that is the "survival of the fittest" process that has kept the fish alive for centuries.

Sardines do not have arms and do not like to hold on to other sardines unless they are in hiding with the lead sardine.

In summary:
- **Go blindly**
- **Say "toy boat" each time you hear "toy boat"**
- **Find the lead sardine**
- **Don't hold on to other fish**
- **Hide with lead sardine and remain silent**

PS A real little known fact: A sardine is any fish that is preserved in oil and used for food. A sardine is not a species of fish.

Sorry Sucker

Sorry Sucker

PROPS:
One plastic pipe per person - 1 inch in diameter approximately 2 1/2 feet long, a table tennis ball

OBJECTIVE:
Move a table tennis ball person to person by sucking the ball to the end of a tube. The activity is a fun icebreaker.

HISTORY:
This activity was created at the 1993 OTRA conference just before I introduced Puff-O-War. Steve Balsters had brought a stack of plastic tubes used for packing material to the conference hoping that someone would find a use for the tubes and take them. Several people played with the tubes like trumpets while others tossed them around. Someone wondered if we could transport things by sucking them to the end of a tube. . . One thing led to another and soon Sorry Sucker was born. It was creative synergy in action. Be prepared for the rude comments that this activity seems to encourage. It makes for a lot of fun.

INSTRUCTIONS:
Beginner's Level-
Stand in a circle with a tube for each of you. Without touching the ball, suck it up with the tube and pass the ball with the tube to the person to your right without letting the ball touch the floor. Try to pass the ball all the way around without dropping it.

Competitor's Level-
Now that we know that we can pass the ball without dropping it, let's go for speed. How quickly do you think we can pass it from tube to tube all the way from beginning to the end?

Expert's Level-
We have gone for quality and speed and now it is time for the test. Stand in a circle, each with your tube. This time the ball must be passed between

your legs. If you drop the ball you're OUT OF THE GAME! and the next person in line is responsible for starting the ball again. Of course if you drop the ball you are not really out of the game. You become a heckler (or sorry sucker) who can move around the circle and harass the other players in hopes of making them join your team by dropping the ball. The sorry suckers cannot make physical contact with the suckers.

When two suckers remain the game is done. Of course they could continue, but they might turn into all day suckers.

The Star

The Star

TIME:
30 minutes

PROPS:
40-50 foot rope tied to itself
to form a large circle

OBJECTIVE:
The whole group creates a five pointed star (the kind that crisscrosses in the middle) with a circle of rope.

HISTORY:
Mary Todd and I presented a workshop of new games and activities to a group at the 1993 Texas Experiential Ropes Association (T.E.R.A.) conference. The workshop started off requiring flexibility. The twelve to fifteen participants we expected turned into approximately forty. I had thought of the star activity, but hadn't tried it until that day. I had imagined using the activity with a smaller group and have since found that it works best with seven to twenty people. It took the conference group a while, but the willing participants finally accomplished their goal.

INSTRUCTIONS:
Ask everyone in the group to grab the rope and get into a circle.

Inform everyone that they cannot let go of the rope or trade places with the people next to them to accomplish this challenging task (although they can slide along the rope).

The goal of this activity is for the whole group to create a five pointed star with the rope (the kind that crisscrosses in the middle as illustrated below).

Once they think the task is complete, ask them to slowly lower the star to the ground and step back to admire their work.

Strategic Tic Tac Toe

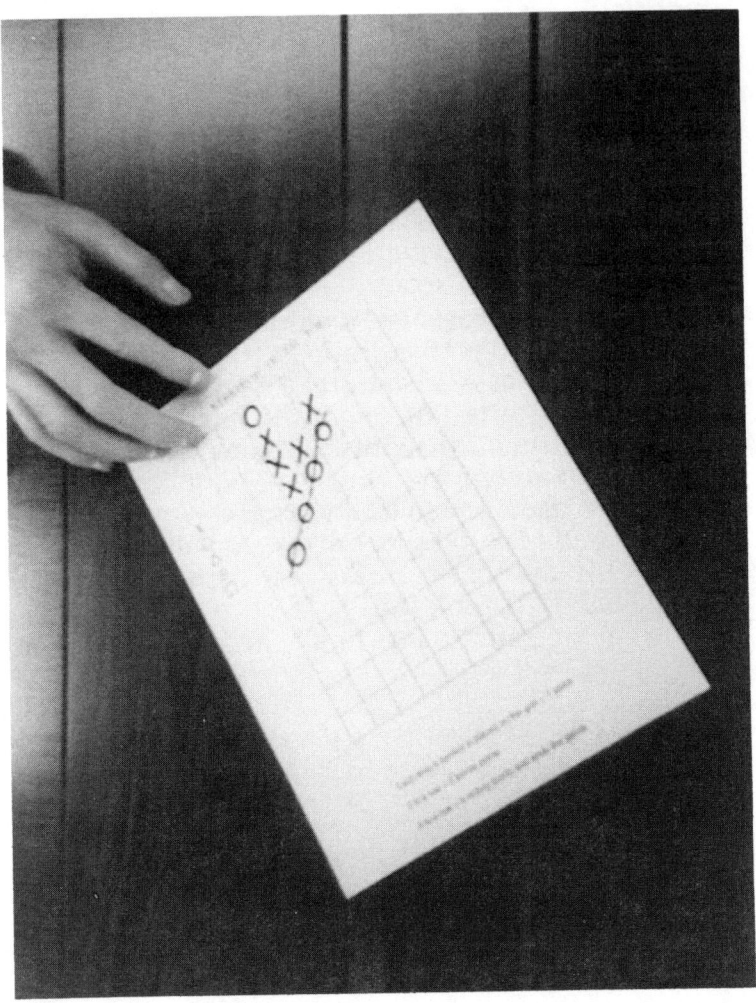

Strategic Tic Tac Toe

PROPS:
Pens of pencils for each participant, two or three copies of the game grid for each set of players.

OBJECTIVE:
Players try to get as many points as they can.

HISTORY:
I thought of this activity while trying to turn some paper and pencil games into life-size activities like the grid. I played it with a friend for a few games. The first game we scored 17 points trying to compete. A few games later we scored 145 points trying to cooperate and the last game we scored 270 points using a "secret" strategy (just try to beat that one). An interesting thing about the games we played was that in the first few games I tried to block my "opponent" after she got three in a row so that she wouldn't win. After we started to cooperate, I would block my "partner" so that she wouldn't get four in a row and end the game by accident.

FACILITATOR'S NOTES:
This activity falls into the competition verses cooperation category. When you present strategic tic tac toe to a group give the instructions clearly and quickly before too many questions can be asked in front of the whole group.

The idea for the first round or two is never to say they are in competition, but usually they are. Just ask everyone to select a symbol and then emphasize the scoring system, especially that four-in-a-row is four victory points and ends the game.

In subsequent rounds, ask for scores from each set of players and announce the totaled score. Maybe reveal a score like 124 as a benchmark. You will see the teamwork light bulbs go off if they haven't already.

If you have time for the teams to try for a record, the 270 point score is the highest I have seen so far.

Scoring can be a paradigm shift for some people. Each symbol on the grid is one point. Three of the same symbols in a row earn you two bonus points. . . so that is one for each of the three symbols plus two more for the bonus. . . five points total. Four consecutive symbols give you four victory points, but each four-in-a-row is made by two overlapping three-in-a-rows (so am I stretching the rules or am I taking advantage of all my options?) so a four-in-a-row is really worth twelve points.

STRATEGIC TIC TAC TOE

X
O
△
S
□

Each time a symbol is placed on the grid = 1 point
3 in a row = 2 bonus points
4 in a row = 4 victory points and ends the game

Get into groups of 2-5 people. Each person should choose a symbol (like regular tic tac toe). Each person should take turns writing a symbol in any empty square on the grid. Object: See how many points you can score. Be sure to stop when 4 like symbols are placed in a row.

Team Belay

Team Belay

"Belay" is a word you might hear around rock climbers. . . or on ropes courses. Whether it is used as a noun, verb or other form, it basically means to keep someone safe. The context in which I use belay refers to a safety system consisting of a climber and a belayer connected by a climbing rope that has been connected to a safety cable on a high ropes course.

Warning: Without proper training and supervision, any ropes course activities (including this one) could result in injury, even death. Please learn the safety procedures before utilizing any climbing event.

The team belay is a technique for belaying a climber that gets several course participants involved in keeping a climber safe on a high ropes course. The technique is quick to teach and safe for the climber. (See the team belay picture.)

The belay team consists of five or more people: A primary belayer, two or more secondary belayers, a rope holder, and an anchor.

The primary belayer pulls the climbing rope through a friction device so that it takes-up the slack in the climber's rope.

The secondary belayers assist the primary belayer by pulling on the rope enough so that it never develops slack between them.

The rope holder gathers the rope so it never touches the ground. Be sure the rope is gathered so that no tangles develop in the rope as the climber is lowered. The facilitator should be the rope holder if there is any prospect that the belayers might become careless. Regardless whether or not the facilitator is the rope holder, each belay team should have direct supervision by an experienced challenge course facilitator.

The anchor holds onto the back of the primary belayer's harness to stabilize him. Sometimes the weight difference between the primary belayer and the climber is enough to cause the primary belayer to lift off the ground a few inches as the climber is lowered.

Make the primary belayer responsible for inspecting the climber's hookup and harness. Also instruct the primary belayer to use commands before the climber ascends.

The whole team should follow under the climber as he makes his way across the high event and then takes up any additional slack in the rope before the climber sits or steps off the element.

While lowering the climber, the all belayers should maintain contact with the rope and let the rope slip through their fingers in a controlled fashion.

Team Blowgun

Team Blowgun

PROPS:
PVC Pipes, PVC fittings, a dart (not pointed), hula hoop

The team blowgun requires at least 14 pieces of pipe (At least 1 pipe should be 2 1/2 feet long or more to provide a barrel.) and 10 "T" fittings for a team of 4-10 people.

If you like a little variation, add some 45 degree fittings to the equipment. . . just make sure you have enough pipe pieces to complete at least one version of the blowgun.

I make a dart with a one inch circle of felt, a one inch length of dowel rod, a small screw, and a six inch string. Use what you have. Some people make the dart with piece of plastic and a small wad of paper.

OBJECTIVE:
Blow a dart into a target.

HISTORY:
I thought of the team blowgun on the way from Tulsa to Estes Park, Colorado in 1993. Three of us drove there for a regional AEE conference. When I had some free time, I slipped away from the conference and purchased some pipe, fittings and a hacksaw blade. An hour later, the prototype was finished. That night I persuaded some friends to try it out in the hallway of our dorm. We laughed so hard I am surprised we weren't asked to leave.

PREPARATION:
Make sure you have all the pieces. Lay out the pieces unassembled.

Mark a firing line and set a hula hoop target approximately 30 feet away.

Clean the pieces in the dishwasher or use a bleach-water solution when you are done with the activity.

Lay out the materials for the team to begin their design and construction.

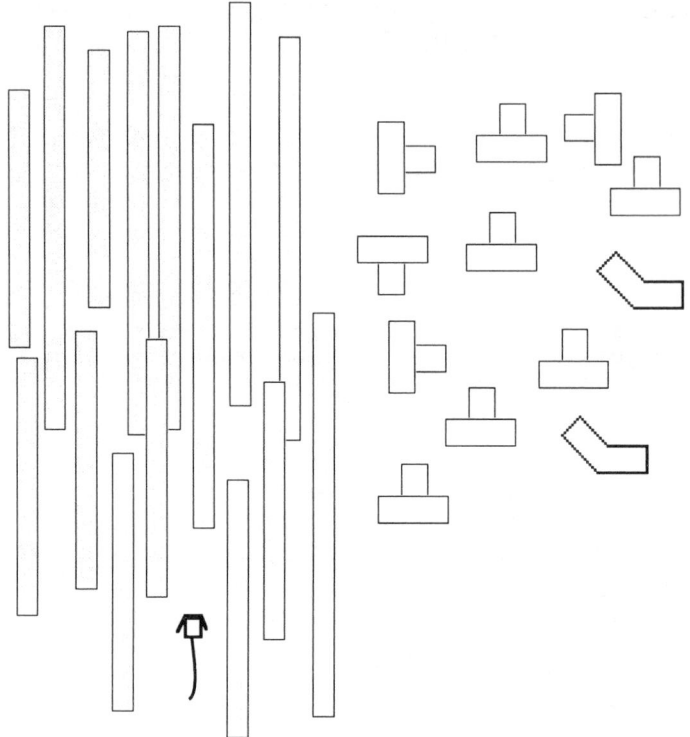

INSTRUCTIONS:

From the materials in front of you, construct a team blowgun that will deliver a dart into the target. The target is 30 feet away.

Nothing can cross the firing line (except the dart, of course).

All the materials must be used in the construction of the blowgun and everyone in the team must be involved in the blowing.

OBSERVATIONS:

This activity is two problem solving activities in one. First the team has to design the blowgun and then they have to figure out how to hit the target.

Some teams have a hard time with this activity because of two commonly misunderstood concepts. 1) If everyone blows at the same time, the air pressure is only as strong as your weakest member. Blow back can occur. 2) Air really can be blown around corners.

Some people question the potential health/sanitation of this game. Truthfully you are at risk of sharing air blown through the tubes, however, many other commonly used activities require close contact with others and their air. This activity is not for every group. Use good judgment before starting into it. If someone is sick in the group, give them another role to play or do a different activity.

Variations:
Go for distance. In a record breaking hurl, a team of ten propelled a dart 74 feet at the 1994 OTRA For Play conference.

Go for accuracy. Draw a target on a piece of flip chart paper with positive and negative scores. Write on the end of the dart with a crayon so that it will mark the paper when it makes contact.

Tower E.G.G. Drop

Tower E.G.G. Drop

PROPS:
Each team of 3-5 people will need the following supplies:

* Variety of egg protection supplies: 30-50 drinking straws, masking tape, six feet of string, chewing gum, scissors, cotton balls, lunch sack, drinking cup, three balloons etc.

* A weight: I use a one foot length of 4X4 lumber but anything approximately two pounds will work.

* Belay equipment for each team.

OBJECTIVE:
Drop an egg, without breaking it, from a high ropes course tower or other high course event.

HISTORY:
The first time we tried this activity, we were working with an oil related business. The participants enjoyed creating the egg protection device and resourcefully developed a way to transport their device across a series of four high events before reaching the 35 foot drop site. Yes, there were survivors.

INSTRUCTIONS:
Read the scenario written below. It communicates much of the detail that I will not repeat here. Give the teams 30 minutes to develop and build their egg protection devices. When the time limit has expired, ask each team to market its device to the rest of the group. After the marketing, everyone should prepare to deliver the eggs to the drop site. Each team will need harnesses, carabiners, etc., to safely belay the team member who is climbing with the egg. The climber drops his team's egg once he reaches the drop site. Since the egg is exposed (see the scenario) it will be easy to inspect for damage.

FACILITATOR NOTES:

The egg drop concept has been widely used in training. Rarely have I heard of drops from such a distance except as a school science project or great stunt. The way the following scenario is set-up, the additional challenge is in getting the unbroken egg to the drop site. The exposed portion of the egg and the added weight increase the perception (and maybe some reality) of risk to the team's mission.

I would suggest using a team belay. Caution people not to stand directly under the climbers since they will be carrying a weight that could fall prematurely.

TOP SECRET

Background:

For years fuel has been transported by pipelines in some form or another. A recent discovery in the field of fuel transportation has opened a whole new range of customers that include many remote countries around the world. The invention of a powerful new fuel packaging system has allowed researchers to concentrate fuels 986%. The new fuel containers (the Excellent Gas Geronimators) are lightweight and resistant to the highly corrosive nature of the concentrated fuel. Unfortunately, the Excellent Gas Geronimators are very fragile and will crack or open if impacted.

Your Mission:

Design and build a protective structure to allow the E.G.G. to safely supply fuel to locations currently inaccessible by traditional methods. The new fuel containers will be air dropped to the customers. You will have 10 minutes of design time and 20 minutes to build and practice marketing your design. Once the structures are built and marketed, you will test them at the drop site.

You will be building your designs and testing them in conditions similar to a real delivery.

A successful design will ensure your company leadership in the world marketplace and each of you a significant bonus.

Fuel Container Specifications:

* Fuel container (E.G.G.) must free-fall the entire drop height

* Some portion of the E.G.G. must protrude from the protective device so that the fuel is accessible immediately upon delivery.

* Wind conditions will be a factor in supplying the fuel to future customers, so a weight (provided) must be incorporated into the protective structure.

* Only the approved building materials can be used in the fuel container's protective structure. These materials will be provided.

Ideal Conditions:

Competitors are currently designing similar structures around the world. Our product must be better built and better marketed. A strong structure that is easy to mass produce and uses as few materials as possible will be ideal.

Transporting Quality To The Source

Transporting Quality To The Source

TIME:
30 min - 1 1/2 hours Time depends mostly on how often the team repeats steps 3 & 4.

PROPS:
Gather a variety of containers, things that liquid can temporary transported with like sponges, Nerf balls, pipe pieces, spoons, wooden trim, buckets, cups (with 1-3 holes punched in them), cones, plastic. . . you get the picture. You also need a marker, such as a spot for each participant and two identical containers that will each hold approximately quart of water.

OBJECTIVE:
Transport a specific volume of water from person to person and see how much really can make it to the end.

HISTORY:
Steve Balsters and I were brainstorming ways to make a gap analysis and flow charting class more fun. He mentioned the idea of getting something through a process that had many "right ways" to do it. The ideas started flowing and soon we had this activity roughed out. I tried the activity for the first time three months later and it was very powerful for the group. Everything went well except that I had given them a gallon of water and it was just too much with the tools they had to work with.

PREPARATION:
Arrange a semicircle of markers (one for each participant) five feet apart on the ground. Collect your props and pile them a few feet from the markers. Take the two identical containers (e.g., coffee pots) and fill one of them with water (fill it to a certain mark). Place the filled container at one end of the line of markers and the empty container at the other.

SCENARIO:

You have been chosen by the Federal Government as one of 20 sample teams in the United States to demonstrate quality, efficiency, and effectiveness. They have guaranteed widespread communication of the results to the public.

Your task involves step by step instructions that must be followed in sequence. Each step must be completed before the next step is revealed.

Step 1   Each person in the team should select one tool from the pile of equipment then stand on one of the markers placed in a semicircle.

Step 2   Without stepping from your marker, transport all the team's liquid from the container through the line of people into the container on the other end of the line by using the tools you selected. Tools cannot be traded in this step. The containers on the ends cannot be moved from the ends.

Step 3   Compare the volume of water you started with to the volume you finished with. If there is much of a difference, stop and use your problem solving methods to improve the process.

Step 4   Return to Steps 1-3 and try the process until the team is satisfied with the results. Later this year your scores will be published with the other 19 companies in a comparative study.

Step 5   Record what made the team successful. Be specific.

Step 6   Celebrate!

Trolley Journey

Trolley Journey

PROPS:
- Four envelopes
- Scissors
- Trolleys - a pair of boards with rope handles, large enough for the whole team
- Bandannas, one for each participant
- Journey scenario
- Appropriate quote

OBJECTIVE:
A team uses trolleys to make its way from point A to point B gathering instructional notes as they travel.

HISTORY:
I have used the trolleys in teambuilding sessions for as long as I have known how to train experientially. Usually, the team hears a scenario and begins a trek using their strange shoes in the process.

Recently I wrote this journey for an energetic team as an opening activity for their three-day training session. I liked the way it kept me out of the action while the team traveled to each envelope. I was able to step back and assess the group's dynamics from a distance instead of being in the middle of the action.

From the team's perspective, if something could go wrong, it did. They all made it to the end after an hour of struggle. Finally everyone was cured of their ailments. The activity focused the group quickly and set a good tone for the rest of the experience.

PREPARATION:
Cut a quote into five puzzle pieces.

Cut the journey scenario into pieces and place parts 1-4 in envelopes and a quote piece with each part.

Place a set of trolleys at the start of the journey with the "welcome" note.

Put the envelopes approximately 15 feet apart between the start and the end of the journey. Make sure they can be easily seen by the participants.

Place the final note and the last quote piece at the end of the journey.

FACILITATOR'S NOTES:

Because of the muscle used in this particular activity, it is a good idea to do some stretches with the group before they begin. Along those lines, I would suggest that any consequences for stepping off the trolleys effect their verbal communication rather than their physical ability to traverse. It will be a long journey even with all of their arms, legs, and eyesight.

The quote I have provided is more funny than inspirational. Choose any quote that seems appropriate to your situation. The quote provides a "lesson" at the end of the journey and is meant only to be an interesting extra.

Welcome!

Ahead is a journey of many decisions, challenges, consequences, and rewards.

A recent attempt to rid the area of unwanted insects ended in tragedy. The experimental genetically engineered chemical was mixed at 445 times its recommended strength and has caused the ground to react strangely with human skin, clothing, and behavioral responses.

Using the materials in front of you, somehow make your way safely to the _____. Stepping from the protective boards will effect your body in one of a variety of ways such as Little Caesar's disease (everything you say, you repeat). Your facilitator has been trained to diagnose your particular reaction to the chemical. Be careful!

Several markers along your path will give you vital insights into a cure. On your journey remind yourselves of the skills that will accomplish your task and the skills that will benefit the entire team during and after the journey.

Several situations will be written on notes at the markers. Decisions about these situations should be made by the entire team.

#1

If the entire group has traveled together as one team on the equipment, one person is temporarily immune to the chemical's effects for 5 minutes but the immunity only works while the person is in physical contact with the team.

-or-

If the group has left some of its team members behind, two people are blind.

#2

If everyone's ideas have been listened to by the team one person is temporarily immune to the chemical's effects for 5 minutes but the immunity only works while the person is in physical contact with the team.

-or-

If ideas have not been listened to or some team members have dominated the group's decisions, 2 people must turn around and face away from the destination while they travel.

#3

If adequate planning occurred prior to the start of your journey all current handicaps are cured.

-or-

If planning was too hasty or non-existent prior to the start of the journey, 4 arms are completely paralyzed.

#4

If the team has been honest about its actions and answers to the previous statements on the journey, all handicaps are cured and one person is temporarily immune to the chemical's effects for 5 minutes, but the immunity only works while the person is in physical contact with the team.

-or-

If the integrity of the team was at any time less than it could be, all members of the team are mute.

-or-

If the team has avoided all handicaps up to this point, everyone is temporarily immune to the chemical's effects for 5 minutes but the immunity only works while everyone is in physical contact with each other.

Welcome to the end of first leg of your continuing journey. The chemical has been neutralized by a combination of your teamwork and time. All handicaps have been cured by divine intervention. Read aloud your completed quote.

Assertiveness

If you want action, let people know what is expected of them. For example, there's the story of the museum guide who was just finishing the tour, saying: "And here, ladies and gentlemen, at the close, this splendid Greek statue. Note the noble way in which the neck supports the head, the splendid curve of the shoulders, and, ladies and gentlemen, note the natural way in which the open hand is stretched out, as if to emphasize: 'Don't forget a tip for the guide.' "

Maxwell Droke

Trust Scavenger Hunt

Trust Scavenger Hunt

PROPS:
One bag per small group. Heavy cloth bags or large grocery sacks work well.

OBJECTIVE:
Small teams find objects in the surroundings and another team tries to identify each of the objects by feeling of them.

HISTORY:
With many of the smaller groups I have worked with, I run into the need for new trust activities that can be played indoors. This was the case when I worked with a treatment staff in Bartlesville, Oklahoma a few years ago. They had already experienced many of the more common events so pulled this one out of the air and it worked! Necessity really is the mother of invention.

INSTRUCTIONS:
Divide the group into an even number of smaller groups of threes or fours.

Each small group has 15 minutes to gather four objects to put into their team's bag. There are some basic requirements. The objects must fit into the bag and one object must be old, one must be new, one must be borrowed, and one must be purple (just kidding. . . it has to be blue).

Teams are not supposed to see what other teams gather.

When the 15 minutes have expired, the small teams gather and exchange guesses. Pair one team with another and ask each pair of teams go at the same time if you have multiple teams. A person from one team reaches into another team's bag and feels one of the objects and makes a specific guess, pulls the object out, and everyone on the two small teams judges for accuracy. Then someone from the other team takes a turn at guessing the identity of an object from the other team's bag. The paired teams take turns until all the objects are identified.

If you are the competitive type, develop a scoring system for the activity.

OBSERVATIONS:

If trust is dependent on risk or perceived risk, this activity can easily be called a trust activity. Teams will often scheme (plan) before they head out on their hunt. People often joke about finding something disgusting to put into their bag, but they rarely follow through.

The facilitator can easily influence the tone of this activity. Be aware of how you instruct and explain the game. If it's just for fun, play it up and encourage everyone to be creative and use their 15 minutes. If it is more serious, preframe what behaviors effectively create trust among people and challenge the teams to try it out.

Be aware that if you do this activity inside around offices, everyone on the floor may be disturbed by scavengers looking for unique objects to bag. It's a lot of fun.

Vortex with a Twist

Vortex with a Twist

OBJECTIVE:
Create a meaningful quick closure that metaphors a teambuilding experience.

HISTORY:
In early 1994, Mary Todd and I were training a team near Colorado Springs. We had worked with the team before and they had completed a Quality orientation for their whole company. This session was a chance for them to learn some more activities and have fun. Just before the close of our time together, some of the team members announced they were needing to leave the team. It was an emotional time. I had been thinking of new twists on familiar closures. This one was just right. The Vortex (from More New Games, p. 175) has always been one of my favorites. With the addition of a twist at the end, we all felt a little closer in many ways.

INSTRUCTIONS:
Everyone holds hands in a circle, facing the center. The facilitator drops hands with the person on his right and leads the line clockwise around the inside of the circle. The person who was to the right of the facilitator stays stationary until the line flips him about and the facilitator holds his free hand again. Everyone should be facing outward holding hands. Ask everyone to remain holding hands and slowly turn around and face the center again. The resulting circle will be much smaller and have everyone's arms crossed in front of them.

To add intensity and meaning to this closure, verbally lead the group through the activity: "We have all been focusing inward during the last few days while we have been demonstrating how to be effective as a team. Now we will be traveling back into the environment we left for a while." Ask everyone to say something positive to each person as they pass in the circle. Slowly lead the group around and complete the circle again, facing outward. Say, "Now

193

it is time to take what we learned and experienced and use it, but regardless of where we go, let's hope this experience has brought us closer together." Ask everyone to remain holding hands and carefully turn and face the center.

If you want less intensity in your closure, drop hands with the person on your right and start the line clockwise then every few people weave under and outside the circle then under and in side the circle. It spins the pivot people with each weave.

OBSERVATIONS:
When the twist occurs, some people may have trouble turning without letting go of hands. If it happens just tell them to twist the other direction.

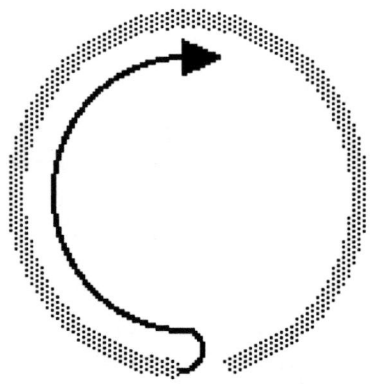

Wampum

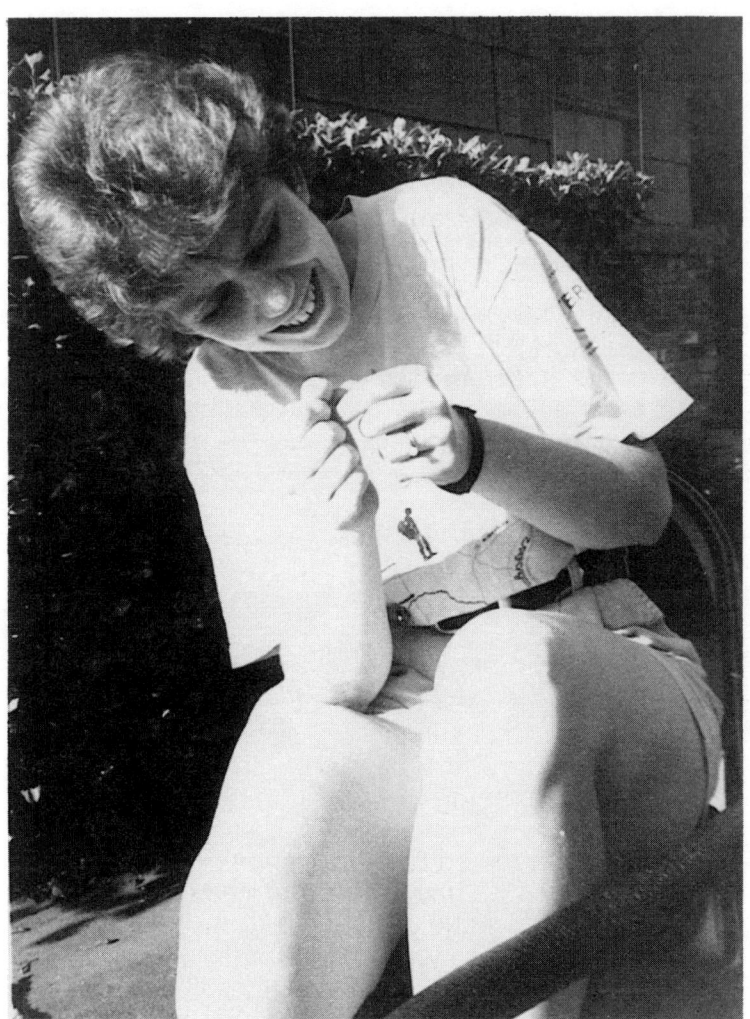

Wampum

PROPS:
A foam sword or a piece of pipe insulation

OBJECTIVE:
To learn everyone's name in a fun activity without being hit with a foam sword.

HISTORY:
I learned this game many years ago when I was a youth director. It was called States because everyone was supposed to pick one state (like Texas) from the fifty. A few years ago I suggested we play the game since I had so much fun with it. Mary told me it was in one of our games books. I looked it up and sure enough, it was in The Bottomless Bag by Karl Rohnke and was called Waumpum. I made up the fun scenario below and we have played it many times since.

SCENARIO:
Many years ago this land was inhabited by several Indian tribes. Disputes between tribes were fairly common, but a war broke out and all the tribes began fighting against each other. It seemed almost under control while the braves were fighting, but it escalated to the point where women, children, and the elderly were being hurt.

Two chiefs recognized the insanity and joined to somehow stop the chaos. With some time and a great deal of effort the chiefs organized a peace meeting to negotiate with all the tribes. A representative from each tribe was asked to sit in a circle with the other representatives. The meeting was going to be tense so something had to be done to reduce the hostility that had been created.

An introduction activity was created called wampum. The game leader would take a nutria* tail and strip the bone from it, then stuff the tail with cotton to form the wampum stick. The warriors would sit in a circle facing one another with the game leader in the middle holding the stick.

When a warrior's name was called the warrior was supposed to avoid being wamped (hit by the wampum stick) by calling out someone else's name from the group. Whoever was named became the next target of the wamper, and so on. A wamp had to be delivered anywhere below the knees. If someone was hit above the knees it was considered an act of war and might spark the conflicts again.

Whenever someone was wamped (before calling out another warrior's name), that person stood in the center of the circle to become the new wamper. The person who was the wamper sat down in the circle and had three seconds to call someone's name or he became the target of the new wamper.

The activity became a common way to begin peaceful negotiations. Even today you can hear references to the game as people trade goods and services. In the spirit of keeping with that peace tradition, try the game and see what you think.

* A nutria is a real animal that lives in the rivers, lakes and streams of America. It resembles a beaver except that its tail is like that of a rat.

OBSERVATIONS:

Wampum is a fast activity for learning new names. It usually starts off slowly until people fully understand the rules and the strategies.

Before playing with a group of strangers, ask everyone to share his/her name once or twice. If you are playing with a group that knows each other, I would suggest asking everyone to think of a unique animal name and use those instead of their real names.

I have also used this activity to review training concepts from a previous session. Each person was supposed to say, in a word or short phrase, a key concept he remembered from the session before.

The words or short phrases became their game names.

Speaking of strategy. . . if you (the facilitator) remember two names and focus on calling just one of those names when your name is called, you can stay out of the middle longer. I suggest two names because if you call wamper's name, you're still the target!

To end the game, get wamped and go back to the middle.

... about
Learning
Unlimited
Corporation

Imagine This . . . . . .

"Good morning, Class! Today we are going to learn to ride a bicycle. After the 'How to Ride a Bicycle' video, we will be completing pages 24 - 48 of your workbook. A short break will be followed by small group discussions on the importance of riding bicycles. We will complete the training with an action planning process to transfer the skills you learn today into your job."

Learning to be a team is like learning to ride a bicycle.

Did you learn to ride a bicycle in a classroom???

Learning Unlimited Corporation (LUC) puts work groups on the "teamwork" bicycle.

LUC provides classroom concepts as the foundation for the <u>real</u> learning:
GROUPS BECOME TEAMS BY BEING TEAMS.

Try "Learn by Being"
--
The Learning Unlimited Development Process.

**5155 East 51st, Suite 108
Tulsa, OK   74135**

**(888) 622-4203 toll free
(918) 622-3292
(918) 622-4203 fax**

Experience-Based Training & Development

Assessment
All the training we provide is customized to the specific needs of the customer. Assessment is critical to creating a process that "fits". We strive to build upon effective training which has already occurred or provide proven training guides when the training concepts do not already exist. Surveys, interviews, in-house documents, business plans etc. all provide vital information to make our training "stick".

Customized Training
If you contacted all of our customers and asked them what they did in their training sessions, you would never hear the same schedule repeated. We are serious when we say the training is customized. We have designed programs for 30 minutes to 70 hours and for two to 3000 people at a time.

Follow-up and Evaluation
Follow-up sessions are scheduled with customers to provide ongoing support. Evaluation by means of pre and post assessments verifies the effectiveness of the training in terms of interpersonal and bottom line measures.

Consultation

We enjoy designing and implementing training. We also consult to the design of in-house training programs and organizational development.

The range of our training includes:

People Skills
- Effective Communication
- Negotiation
- Leadership Development
- Conflict Management
- Behavioral Styles
- Diversity
- Creativity
- Dealing with Change
- Trust
- Coaching
- Feedback

Task Skills
- Process Improvement
- Decision Making Tools
- Measurement
- Effective Meetings
- Goal Setting
- Strategic Planning
- Vision/Mission Creation

Trainer Skills
- Icebreakers
- Games & Initiatives
- Facilitator Training
- Training Design
- Ropes Course Training
- Handling Difficult Situations

. . . about
The
Author

Sam has a Master's Degree in Industrial/Organizational Psychology from the University of Tulsa, and a Bachelor's Degree in Psychology from Texas Tech University in Lubbock.

Sam trains, facilitates, and speaks nationwide in a variety of corporate and educational settings including Fortune 500 companies, small businesses and universities. Best known for his creativity, Sam has trained groups of as few as two people and as many as three thousand. He certifies Ropes Course facilitators and develops related indoor and outdoor training activities for adults. He is active in organizations such as the Association for Experiential Education, American Society for Training and Development, and the Tulsa Area Human Resources Association. In 1996, Sam was recognized as "Practitioner of the Year" in a five-state region for his achievements in training by the Association for Experiential Education.

His other published materials include the book <u>50 Ways To Use Your Noodle</u>, a <u>S.T.A.T.S. Test,</u> and <u>Indoor Games For College Students And The Extremely Bored</u>.

Ordering More

Books and Game Equipment for any of the activities within this book may be ordered directly by the following:

calling - (918) 622-3292 or (888) 622-4203

faxing - (918) 622-4203

writing -   5155 East 51st, Suite 108
               Tulsa, OK 74135

e-mail -   ssikes@npi.net

internet -   www.learningunlimited.com

Cover Design:
Jim Weems
AdGraphics
Text and Layout:
Skia font
Microsoft Word 5.1
Macintosh PowerBook 520c
Photography:
Sam Sikes (with a lot of help and trust from some friends)

....

A sincere thanks goes to the teams that motivated the creation of the activities listed below.

Amoco IT Center
Sardines Scenario
Barbarian Golf
Cascia Hall
Quick Mathematical Division
Citgo Petroleum Corporation
Trolley Journey
Three-Way Grid
Lincoln Property Company
Photo Finish
Pikes Peak Mental Health Center
On Target - For Larger Team on Zip Line
Transporting Quality To The Source
Vortex with a Twist
Phillips Petroleum Company
On Target - For Smaller Team on High Course
QuikTrip Corporation
Feeding the Zircon Gorilla
Shadow Mountain Institute
Quality Journey
Trust Scavenger Hunt
Southwestern Power Administration
Balloon Castles
T D Williamson Inc.
Lines of Communications
TransOk Inc.
On Target - For Smaller Team on Zip Line
Tower E.G.G. Drop
United Video Inc.
Easy. . . Knot!